LOST ALONG
THE WAY

LOST ALONG THE WAY

Life, Loves, CEOs, and LBOs

MICHAEL RAYMOND YOUNG

Grateful acknowledgment is made to the following for permission
to use and/or quote from copyrighted material: **Condé Nast** for
cartoon *"Perhaps we could find a way to redefine 'profit.'"*; **Universal
Uclick** for cartoon *Arlo & Janis*; **Hal Leonard Corporation** for songs
High Noon, I Wouldn't Have Missed It for the World, and *Summertime*;
Alfred Publishing for songs *High Noon, Summertime,* and *Once Upon a
Time*; and **Music Sales West** for song *La vie en rose.*

International Standard Book Number: 978-0-578-17645-1

Library of Congress Control Number: 2016900827

Illustrations by Kip Ayers

Cover design, book design, and layout by Jim L. Friesen

Printed in the United States of America by Mennonite Press, Inc.,
Newton, Kansas. www.MennonitePress.com

For the loves
in my life

Contents

Kansas prairie grain silo

A lifetime lived, and then forgotten?

GONNA happen, gotta happen, for most of us anyway. Okay, maybe a few of us will carve out our own space on Google, but unless you've got a name like Napoleon, Einstein, or Roosevelt, don't bet on it.

That's why this book was written. When I'm gone I want to leave behind some small trace of my existence.

Hope it's not just an egocentric need that has pushed its way to the surface. Hope it's more the need that we all have not to be forgotten.

Michael Raymond Young

Illustrations

ALL illustrations in this book were custom-drawn for the purpose of conveying a visual sense of the story presented. The vast majority of these illustrations were created by Kip Ayers, a freelance digital illustrator living in upstate New York. He works primarily in the publishing industry but welcomes a challenge in any genre. When he can muster the strength to pull himself away from his work, he spends his time hiking, playing guitar and Native American flute, and marveling at nature's flawless artistic technique.

It was the author's very good fortune to have worked with an artist of such exceptional talent, work ethic, dedication, and pleasant disposition.

www.kipayersillustration.com
kip@kipayersillustration.com

CHAPTER 1

How in the Hell Did I Get Here?

IT'S Saturday, July 5, 1:20 p.m., and I'm in El Dorado, Kansas, on an absolutely beautiful summer's day. How in the hell did I get here? I'm a Michigan boy; my address is 724 South Edison. I live with my mom and dad and my brother in a small three-bedroom, one-bath home, which is only a stone's throw away from the Hollywood supermarket. Actually, I used to think that we lived in a somewhat upper-end home and that the Hollywood market was a really big deal. It would only become apparent to me a few years later that some homes actually had more than one bath and that the Hollywood market was a tiny speck of a neighborhood grocery store. But then I'm getting ahead of myself; I live in Royal Oak, Michigan, and the kids in the neighborhood are all outside getting ready to play touch football in the street in front of my home. The curbs are out of bounds, the parked cars are great at blocking out the defenders when you're trying to catch a pass, and extra points are made by kicking the football over the low-hanging wire that runs across the street and past my home. There probably isn't anything that I enjoy more than playing football with the neighborhood gang. I've got to get out there right away.

The only thing I don't like about these summer days is that they end too quickly. You just can't get everything done before it's time to come in for supper. By the time you've ridden your bike past "the stores past the park," played a few innings of pickup baseball, and swum at Salt Water Pool, the day is over. It's just not right, and besides that, the summer is flying by. We'll be back in school before you know it. I really hate school. Well, at least I'll be able to get into an interesting conversation with Mom after Dad heads off for his night school classes. All I have to do is say, "Ma, let's talk." She definitely knows a lot more about things than Dennis's mother or Bob's mother or any of my aunts or uncles. I wonder how she got to be so smart.

I remember once she asked me, "Which do you think you would rather be, the president of a smaller company or the vice president of a large company?" You know what, Ma, I'm not even sure what a president or vice president is, can you explain that to me? Dad's not a president or a vice president, is he? Is that why you and Dad are always fighting about money? I'm worried about our money; do we have to move if we don't have enough money to pay for the house? You know that I watch the gas pump when Dad fills up the car? If it's less than four dollars that's good, but I really get worried when it's more than four dollars because Dad might not have that much. Three sixty? I feel a lot better now.

I was excited when we got to go downtown one Saturday to see where Dad works. That was a big deal for a seven-year-old. There wasn't anyone except us at his office so it was kind of spooky. All the desks were lined up in rows in a large room and around the outside were separate offices. Which one of the offices is yours, Dad? I don't understand, you don't have an office? You sit at that desk? Way over there? Who sits in the offices, the presidents and the vice presidents? You're not a president or a vice president, are you, Dad? I want to go now; is it okay if we go now?

I'm not sure why I feel this way but I think it's better to be one of the bosses. They tell everyone else what to do and they don't have to worry about money. I wonder if that's why Dad quit his job in that big office and started his own bookkeeping service. I know he's the boss now, but Mom and Dad are fighting constantly because we still don't have enough money. Just a second, the phone's ringing.

Hello? Okay, I'll tell him. Dad, some man called and said, "Tell your old man to pay his bills." I'm not going to tell Mom or Dad but I'm scared. I think something is really wrong.

You know, when I grow up I'm going to be different from my dad. They're not going to boss me around and make me scared. No they're not; no they're not; no they're not! I'm going to do all the things that I want to do, and they won't be able to stop me. No they won't; no they won't; no they won't! I think you have to learn how to take care of yourself; it seems like you have to learn to take care of yourself. I'm going to learn how to do that. Hey, Ma, let's talk. Can you tell me what a president is? What's better, Ma, to work for a big or a small company? You know, Ma, I never asked you the question, but I was wondering if there are any other jobs in a company besides a president or a vice president. Probably not.

Maybe things will be different when my dad finishes night school and passes the bar examination. It seems like he's been going to school at night for so long; he'll probably have a lot more time to be with me and Gordy when he's done. I wonder if that's why he doesn't talk to me as much as Mom does. I know he's really busy studying all night long in the back room of our house.

Mom said that this morning's Sunday edition of the newspaper will have a list of everyone who passed the bar examination that dad took several months ago. I guess that's the way you find out if you passed or failed the exam. Can't wait to get the news; I think Mom and Dad will be happy and if they're happy then I'll be happy too. Does it always take this long for the paper to be delivered?

Finally, there's the paperboy and my dad's gone out to meet him on the front porch. Man, this is exciting. Open the paper, Dad. I guess you have to look in the right section to find the names. There's the list; look at all those names. Where's your name, Dad; which one is your name, Dad? Dad?

Mom said that Dad just barely missed passing the exam and that he could request that one or two of his answers to questions be regraded. He only needed a few more points to pass so I could never understand why he didn't at least try; I don't think Mom understood it either. But a year or so later Dad would have another chance to take the exam and that's what he did. That was the same year that I came down with polio and I knew from what Mom had told me that Dad wasn't able to study for the exam like he had wanted to. As we waited again for the Sunday-morning paper I remember feeling a bit uncomfortable and scared but I wasn't sure why. Is your name there, Dad? Dad?

The more time between school and an exam, the more you forget, at least that's what Mom said. So when Dad took the bar exam for the third time he was pretty rusty, at least that's what Mom said. You know I wasn't looking forward to that Sunday morning. I'm not sure, but it might have been a rainy and overcast day, at least that's how I remember it. When the paperboy finally showed up, I wasn't sure why Dad went out to greet him. Dad?

You know something, they're not going to boss me around and make me scared; I'm going to do all the things I want to do and they're not going to stop me; it seems like you have to learn to take care of yourself.

Damn it, riding this bike ain't gettin' me where I need to go; with a car I'd be totally free to do all the things I want to do. Don't tell me about age twenty-one, that's not the moment of liberation; age sixteen is where it all begins. But I won't be old enough to get a driver's license for another few years. Is there anyone on this earth who is suffering more than I am right now? I don't think so. Better start saving for my car. Cut your front grass for seventy-five cents, Mrs. Green, and I'll do the front and back for a dollar fifty. I'll haul that stack of old newspapers out to the trash for fifty cents, sir. Let's see, how much do I have saved up now?

Sure, Mom, you can borrow that three hundred dollars; it's okay, I'm still a couple of years away from buying my car.

Just a couple of months to go and I'll finally be sixteen. Think I'll buy that '53 Chevy convertible now and park it in the driveway until I get my license. Never seen a sweeter-looking car in all my life. And I'm going to apply for that job at Food Fair Market now, so that I'll be able to start work on the day I turn sixteen. The produce department? Pays a dollar twenty-five per hour? Regular stock boys only make a dollar per hour, don't they? Sure, I'll take it. I can't believe it but my sixteenth birthday falls on a Sunday so I'll have to wait one more day to get my license. What time does the driver's license office open Monday morning? Why is my foot shaking on the clutch pedal? That never happened before; must be really nervous taking this driving exam. I passed? Oh my god, this is the best day of my life. Rosanna? Got it. Pick you up at eight.

I sure have learned a lot in the last few years. Wish there was something that I could do, though, to make Mom and Dad happier. I'm starting to feel like I shouldn't have been so hard to get along with for so many years, but then again I had the right to do whatever I wanted to do. There's bound to be trouble if someone tries to tell you what to do, right? That seems right, anyway. Well, it's probably okay to tell people certain things, like don't smoke. Yeah, I am glad they told us not to smoke; sure wouldn't want to have a cough like Dad's. Seems to be getting worse all the time and now he's got a sore chest too.

Dad has lung cancer? An operation? Sorry I was so difficult for so long, Dad. You seem to be recovering from the operation but now you're beginning to lose your balance when you stand. Brain cancer? Sure, Gordy and I will be happy to help you clean out your office. Steady, Dad, leave those things for Gordy and me; we'll take care of everything. Do you know what, Dad? This is the saddest day of my life. I'm standing out back behind your office, and I'm watching you try to get back into the car, and I know you're dying, and I can't do anything to help you, and I want to help you, but there's nothing I can do. Sorry I was so difficult for so long, Dad. Dad?

And I miss you too, Mom. Sure was a role reversal when you were lying helpless in bed and we had to tend to your every need. I miss not being able to talk. If you could just come back for a little while I could tell you all about presidents and vice presidents and how I've learned to take care of myself… just like you said. Sorry I was so difficult for so long, Mom.

I know that one day I'll write down all this, and a lot more, so that it's not forgotten. No one may care, no one may read it, but I know I'll write it down. Maybe I'll follow an introductory piece with snippets of family stories and life experiences that will highlight a few of the more interesting aspects of our family life. There's so much to tell that I better get started right away. You never know what the future holds. I could even end up in Kansas someday.

Chapter 2
And Your Ma Is Good Lookin'

Life was so simple then. All I had to do was climb up on Ma's lap and let her rock me to sleep while she sang some of the most beautiful songs that I have ever heard. At first there was no one else in our world, since my dad's return from the army had been delayed until somewhat after the war's end, and my brother was too small to matter much in my world.

One song that she repeatedly sang was "When Johnny Comes Marching Home Again," even after my dad, whose name was John, had long since come marching home. But it took him a long time to break into that closed world that I shared with my mother. At first he scared the hell out of me; who was this man who was trying to come between me and my ma? Ice cream cones, walks around the block, throwing the ball back and forth…none of that was going to work.

No, you can't come into our world. That's just for Ma and me; stay out!

Okay, Ma, can you sing that "summertime" song again? You know, the one that goes:
...Oh, your daddy's rich and your mamma's good lookin',
so hush, little baby. Don't you cry
...One of these mornings, you're going to rise up singing.
Then you'll spread your wings and you'll take to the sky.
But until that morning, there's a nothing can harm you,
with daddy and mammy standing by.

I always liked the way you sang "and your ma is good lookin'" with extra emphasis. You knew you were good-looking, didn't you, Ma? And I knew, even then, that you were singing about your-self...but just for me. That was something that just you and I had

together, wasn't it, Ma? That was the world we lived in. Us, and no one else.

That was a formative time of life. A magical time, a safe and secure time. Life was all ahead of me then.

But, you said, get ready to "spread your wings and take to the sky," because daddy and mammy won't always be standin' by. Dad…Mom…

A formative time, not just a time when something exceptional happened. There were plenty of those exceptional times, but the truly formative times can probably be counted on two hands. They don't come with an asterisk, and they are not underlined in red, but when you look back on your life you can probably pick them out with relative ease.

Buzzzzz…buzzzzz…buzzzzz…school's out. Third grade sure is boring. Can't wait to visit my special place on the way home. I sure hope that it will work today. I just love that fantastic feeling that I get when it does happen.

I'll walk part of the way home with the other kids but then, about halfway home, I'll head off on my own to my special place. No one else can come, in fact no one else even knows about my special place. I don't tell anyone about it, not even Mom.

There it is, in that big field with all the trees and shrubs and grass. That one enormous shrub has an opening that's just like a cave inside. No one's around, no one can see me, no one knows I'm here. Just push those branches back and then let go of them once I'm inside. I love it here.

Oooooh…I'm heading off…it's working…what a great feeling…every part of me is floating…I'm very happy…I can be anything I want to be…everything I ever wanted is right here, right now…oh, ooh, oooh…I don't want this to ever end…too good to end…ooooh noooo…I'm coming back…I don't want to come back yet…noooo…not yet…just give me one more minute…just one more minute…

Dreaming? Daydreaming? Or was it a hypnotic state? I didn't understand it; in fact, I never even questioned it until I was much older. An out-of-world experience that literally had me in a trance. Words cannot describe the feeling, but I can say without exaggeration that it was the best feeling I've ever had.

Maybe it worked for about a year; maybe it wasn't even that long. And it didn't work every time I tried it; maybe half the time. And then it hardly worked at all. And then it didn't work anymore.

Now, more than sixty years later, if I could have only one wish granted, I'd choose to go back to that place. But I can't get there now. Maybe drugs would work, but I've never, ever done that for good reason: I'd probably never choose to come back.

I don't know what it was about age eight that caused that time in my life to be so formative. We had already been living in our first new home for two years. The neighborhood gang of kids that I hung out with for years had already come together. Football in the streets and baseball in the park were part of the regular routine. And, of course, I had found my special spot under the large shrub in the field that was more or less on the way home from school.

What was it that made that such a special time? Everything seemed to register on the Richter scale with me.

And so it was on that hot summer Sunday in 1952 when Dad said he wanted to take us to see the movie *High Noon* at the wide-screen theater in downtown Detroit. Dad said it was supposed to be a great movie. Couldn't wait; I was sure we were going to have lots of fun.

The movie had hardly started, but I was already hooked. Listen to the melody of that song. Those are killer words; never heard anything like it before:

Do not forsake me, oh, my darlin',
On this, our wedding day.
Do not forsake me, oh, my darlin',
Wait; wait along.
The noonday train will bring Frank Miller.
If I'm a man I must be brave
And I must face that deadly killer
Or lie a coward, a craven coward,
Or lie a coward in my grave.

And look at that Lee Van Cleef character; now there's a bad guy if I've ever seen one.

I was transformed. I was in another world. I'd never heard a melody like that. I'd never heard words to a love song like that. I'd never seen such a consummate bad guy; just look at that weasel face. "I only know I must be brave…," oh man. Three minutes in and I already sensed that this would be the best movie I'd ever seen.

Got that one right! Nothing else ever came close.

You know, it wasn't the first time I'd been exposed to things as they were in real life, but it seemed to be the first time a lot of it registered. There were some very bad guys out there; other guys were very brave. Some music could convey a haunting message and just knock you over. Citizens in your town might turn their back on you just when you need them most. There were some beautiful women in the world, and Grace Kelly was one of them.

The sounds of a loudly ticking clock and a train whistle can mingle with the rhythm of your thumping heart. And when the shootin's all over, and the unsupportive townspeople come out on the street to gather around you, you take off your marshal's badge and throw it at your feet in disgust.

It was a time of awakening: I would be eight years old in another month and things were changing fast for me. At any other time, at any other age, the whole thing might have been nothing more than a fun day at the movies. But it turned out to be a mesmerizing moment, a formative moment that has remained vivid in my mind for all of my years.

Chapter 3

Just One More Time, Dad

There I was, sailing through the air, maybe higher and farther than anyone had ever pole-vaulted before. Might have even been a new 1954 world record; if not that, then it had to be close. As I picked up the broken broom handle that was my vaulting stick I heard my dad's voice calling me to come in for supper. Supper? Now? After what I've just accomplished? Can I do it just one more time, Dad? Then I'll be right in, promise.

Okay, Dad's watching, here we go again, one last time. Soaring, flying with the birds, here comes the ground, crash…snap. Oh, does that hurt! Look at my left arm; the wrist is shifted off to the side at least an inch. Dad, I think I broke my wrist.

Hold the upper part of my arm, Dad, while the doc pulls it straight and shifts it over. Painful beyond words and now you tell me I'm going to have to keep this heavy plaster cast on my arm for three months? And summer vacation just started a few days ago. Well, I guess there's nothing I can do about it. At least I'll have something to brag about tomorrow morning with the kids in the neighborhood.

Trying to sleep with this cast on is difficult, but far worse than that is how bad I feel; just like I had the flu. Morning, Mom, I feel really sick. I don't know why this broken arm is making me feel so bad but I'm going to go out with the kids anyway. I've never felt this sick before and it's getting worse and worse; I'm going home. Mom, I'm really, really sick. Can we go to the doctor?

I don't know why everyone seems to be so upset at the doctor's office, especially Mom. She said she had called Dad at work and that he was going to meet us at the doctor's office. Why is he coming here? Boy, that was quick; he's here already.

We're going to Henry Ford Hospital? Why? Why are we going there? Mom, why are you sitting in the back seat with your

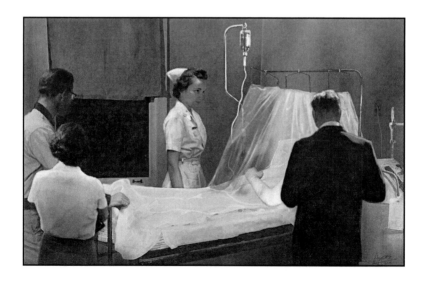

arm around me and why is Dad driving so fast? He's going through all the stoplights; better slow down, Dad, or you'll get a ticket. Why are you crying, Mom?

I've never felt this bad; every part of me hurts worse than ever before. Maybe that's why we've come to this hospital. Just how many of those needles are you going to stick in my arm, anyway? An oxygen tent? Why do I need that? I've never seen so many doctors and nurses in my entire life. Mom and Dad look like they've been crying but they're smiling and telling me everything is okay. A priest is here to talk to me? No, I don't know what the last rites are. Sure, I believe all those things, Father.

Polio, I've got polio. Bulbar polio. The critical phase is over now but I'm going to have to stay in this hospital at least thirty days? You've got to be kidding. Can't get out of bed. Can't eat solid foods other than bananas. What is there to do other than those endless exercises? I sure have come to hate bananas. Hey, there's my brother Gordy. Push this wheelchair around the whole floor again, Gordy, as fast as you can, just like we're at a racetrack.

You and Dad went to see the movie *Shane*? That good, eh? No, it couldn't have been better than *High Noon*; no way! *High Noon* is the best movie ever, Gordy!

Okay, so now it's over. Out of the hospital just in time to start school in the fall. Didn't even miss a term, did I? But never being allowed to play any contact sports again is like a death sentence. You know how much I like football. Touch football is okay but I can't join the Little League team that my dad just started in town. So I'm going to be relegated to the job of water boy for the team. Didn't take long for that demeaning job to get old. I quit! Ninety-four, ninety-five, ninety-six…I'm getting pretty good at this… I wonder what the world record for sit-ups is, anyway. Ninety-seven, ninety-eight…

Chapter 4
Don't Know, Mom

Windsor, Ontario, was just across the Detroit River, so getting our hands on illegal Canadian firecrackers was always easy to do. Can't say we were very original about hiding things when we came back across the border, though. Under the front seat in Dad's car would have been the first place security would have looked if they had chosen to search the car. But we seemed to always be able to get away with it, so there really was no need to get more creative. Anything to declare? No, the kids and I just went across for a Sunday drive. Go ahead. Thanks, Dad.

I'd been fascinated by firecrackers since the age of about five when several older kids who lived in my grandmother's neighborhood used one to blow up a model battleship floating in a small pond. Spectacular, a direct hit; that baby's going down. I was hooked. And now the neighborhood kids and I are the ones who have the firecrackers. Coupled with great imaginations, there were endless ingenious ideas that we were able to come up with.

Let's hammer one end of this old pipe into the ground then drop a large firecracker into the open end. Boom! That was great, but why don't we try dropping something into the pipe after we drop the firecracker in? Then it will be just like a gun. Look, this glass marble fits perfectly. Boom! Didn't see the marble come out but it's definitely not still in the pipe. Stay here, guys, I'm going to get my mother's heavy cast iron frying pan and set it on the front edge of these two patio chairs, right over the open end of the pipe. Next time the marble should shatter when it hits the frying pan; that'll be better than just having it shoot up in the air and not see it. Okay, ready? Quick, firecracker in, marble in, frying pan in place, boom! Oh my god, I can't believe it! Blasted a large hole clean through Mom's quarter-inch-thick frying pan. How could a glass marble do that? No, Mom, I haven't seen your frying pan; don't know where you could have put it.

G...u...n...p...there it is, gunpowder. Look at that; right here in this encyclopedia. Potassium nitrate, sulphur, and powdered charcoal. Is that all there is to it? Just mix those three things together and you have gunpowder? In what proportions? Where can you get those things anyway? Says they're available at almost any drugstore; in fact, potassium nitrate is also called saltpeter, a laxative. Now that's really funny, isn't it? Yes sir, all three. No, I'm not sure what Mom and Dad want it for. They just asked me to pick that stuff up. Think I'll have a milkshake while I'm here, too.

So I guess you just mix them together like this, eh? Now let's see what happens if I touch a match to this stuff. Poof! Did you see that? It worked! I can hardly believe that it's so simple. Now let's try slightly different proportions; a little more potassium nitrate, a little less sulphur and charcoal. Poof! Worked even better. Just got to keep track of all the different proportions and see what works best.

So now it all comes down to this. Pour the powder carefully into the pipe. Slowly screw the cap on the end but before you do, be sure that none of the powder got on the threads. Wouldn't want this thing to blow up in my face while I'm screwing this cap on. Okay, now push that wick that you took off the firecracker into that hole that you drilled in the cap.

There it is, finished. I wonder if it will work. Wonder how far I need to stand back from this thing, just to be safe. Here goes.

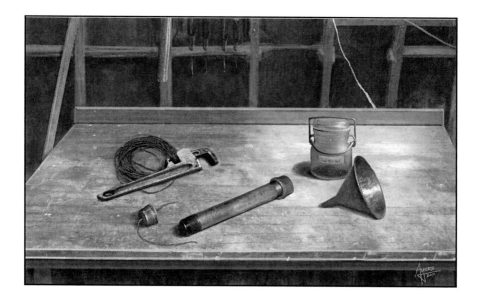

Kaboom! Holy shit, that was like a stick of dynamite! I wonder what will happen if I use a bigger pipe?

Really got this worked out now; know exactly how to do it. Ready to show the kids at St. Benedicts; no eighth graders have ever seen anything like this. Yeah, it's right there on the floor in front of the kneeler, in that bag with my lunch. Why do you think my lunch bag is so big, then? Sure couldn't eat that much, could I? That kid in the pew in front of us keeps kicking my lunch bag whenever he kneels; hey, jerk, stop it. I remember another time when some kid was kicking my lunch like that; my friend and I reached under the pew, grabbed hold of his feet, and pulled him under. Probably not a good idea to do that right now, though; wouldn't want Sister to come over here and snoop around.

I want to show you guys what this baby will do. Where should we put it? I know, in the parking lot, under one of those telephone poles that are laid on their side for cars to pull up to. Okay, light it. Run like hell, you guys. Kaboom! Whump! Oh no! How was I supposed to know that the pole would fly up and hit the underside of that car's bumper, anyway? Let's get the hell out of here; the owner's going to be pissed.

Gonna make the granddaddy of all bombs this time. This one's going to be so powerful that I'll have to bury it way underground to muffle the blast. Trouble is, I won't be able to use a conventional fuse because it will be buried too deep; think I'll try to set it off electrically. If I take one of these flashlight bulbs and carefully break it, I can then insert the filament into the gunpowder in the tube. Then I can attach the filament to a long wire that leads to the back bedroom of my house. When I connect the wires to a battery, the glowing filament should ignite the powder. Let's see…kkkaaabbbooommm!

Did my bomb do that, or did someone just start World War III? I've got a canyon-sized hole in my back yard, the neighbors are all outside wondering what happened, and I can hear police sirens off in the distance. Damn, that was beautiful. Maybe I better lie low for a little while.

Sure wish I'd had as much success building rockets as I did bombs. Thought it was going to be pretty straightforward. Find a lightweight high-strength tube; attach a tapered plug to one end to serve as a nose cone; at the other end fasten a plug with a hole through the center for the nozzle. Fill the tube with gunpowder, aim it straight up, ignite the gunpowder, and…nothing but flames, smoke, and whoosh. There it was, still sitting on the launch pad; hadn't left the ground.

But I was in good company, of course. The US government hadn't been any more successful using rockets to launch satellites than I had been, at least up to that point anyway. One after another they blew up on the launch pad: flames, smoke, and whoosh, but nothing else. Vanguard, Redstone, Atlas, I knew everything about them: their length, diameter, weight, thrust, and payload. The Russians, on the other hand, had even launched a dog into space. What was most troubling, however, was the size of the payloads they were orbiting. Several hundred pounds for the Russians but the satellite that failed to orbit when the US Vanguard blew up weighed only two pounds. Since rocket size and payload are directly related, it was evident that theirs was a lot bigger than ours and that's never a good thing, especially for a guy.

Time after time, failure after failure. Even the US government was starting to have some successes; but not me. And then it happened; sitting right there on the shelf was *Model Rocketry for Amateurs*. Drawings, specifications, formulations, and details that I'd never seen anywhere else. This thing should win an award for best book of the year. I'm sure they'll sell at least a million copies. So it was off to the machine shop that was owned by the father of one of my neighborhood friends. Can you make a nozzle and a nose cone like the ones shown in these drawings, Mr. C ? Will cost that much, eh? Okay, let's do it. Would have thought that I'd get a break on the price; guess that's why he's driving a new Oldsmobile and my old man's not.

But fame and glory would not come so easily. At best my high-tech rockets flew poorly; at worst they stayed on the ground. Nowadays all you have to do is go to a hobby shop and buy a rocket right off the shelf; guaranteed to fly. But what fun is that?

Chapter 5
Get a Job, Son

Daddy wasn't rich, no rich uncles, never played the lottery.

Didn't take a genius to figure out that if I wanted anything more than the bare essentials in life, I was going to have to earn the money it took to get them.

So, Dad, I was wondering if you'll help me buy a car when I turn sixteen in about four years. No, I'm not asking if you'll pay for the whole thing, maybe just half. Not even half, eh? Any help on the insurance, gas, repairs? Well, then how am I supposed to ever get a car? But I'm not old enough to get a job yet; no one would hire me. So you're saying that I could cut other people's grass and do odd jobs? That sounds like hard work…would it be okay then if I used our lawn mower?

Well, I'm finally almost old enough to get a real job; going to turn sixteen in about a month. My friend Don says they're hiring at Food Fair Markets so I think I'll try to get a job there. Hey Don, where did you say the main office is for Food Fair? Man, that's a long way away. Guess I can hitchhike down there, though; that's gotten me almost everywhere else I've wanted to go.

Ride down, sir?…Ride down, sir?…Ride down, sir?…Ride down, sir? Damn it, stranded here at the corner of Six Mile Road and Woodward and I'm going to be late for my job interview at Food Fair. At least there's a center island here at this traffic light. Means you can talk directly to the drivers because you're on their side of the car. Ride down, sir?…Ride down, sir? No? Thanks a lot, man, all I'm asking for is a ride, really appreciate the help…. Ride down, sir?…Ride down, sir? Yes? Thanks. I'm late for a job interview and no one would give me a ride.

Sorry I'm late but no one would…(oh shit, you're the same guy that I just smarted off to a little while ago)…give me a ride. (I might as well turn around and go home; no chance I'm going to

get this job.) Yes sir, that was me. Sorry about that but I was worried about being late for this interview.

What are the odds of that happening? Not only got the job but got the premium job in the produce department. Pays a dollar twenty-five an hour; that's twenty-five cents per hour more than a stock boy makes. Don's going to be pissed to hear that. The produce manager, Murf, is a really cool guy; says he's a tit man; got no use for a big ass; says that all he needs is enough ass to keep his balls from dragging on the bedsheets. Let me think about that for a minute, Murf.

Haven't been on the job long but Murf wants me to close up tonight, by myself. There's a lot to do: take all the chilled things and put them in the cooler; wash down all the racks; sweep and mop the floors. No one's ever done it better; Murf 's going to be impressed when he gets back in the morning. I start at noon tomorrow; when I walk in I'll receive a standing ovation for my closing. Hi, Murf. Well, what did you think of…what do you mean?… I worked hard on that closing…how could it have been *that* bad?"

No sir, Mr. B, I don't know anything about scuba diving but I'm a really hard worker. Been working at Food Fair Markets and they've given me really good reviews. I know that I can do a good job for Water Sports Distributing Company. Yes ma'am, Voight is first-class equipment. It has a two-stage regulator and a purge valve right here on the mouthpiece. On sale for $239. Yes, I'll write that up.

It sure is nice that Mr. B lets us take all of the scuba-diving equipment right off the showroom floor and use it on our days off. Would have never had a chance to learn scuba diving if I had to buy all of this stuff. Do you guys remember last winter when we went to the quarries in Ohio to dive under the ice? Remember how it felt when that ice-cold water ran down the back of our wet suits?

But the time we were deep diving at Stoney Lake was anything but funny. We stirred up the muddy bottom so much that we couldn't see anything in front of us. I got totally disoriented and couldn't tell which way was up, so I continued to swim in the direction that I thought was up. Finally, in a state of total confusion, I decided to pull the cord on the inflatable belt that was hanging loosely at my waist. To my amazement, the inflated belt shot straight off to my side, not in the direction that I thought was up. I hadn't been heading to the surface at all. That was the last time I went diving!

But enough of that. I've got a chance to pick up another sixty-five cents per hour if I can just land that sales job at Dunn's Camera. Mr. C, I've got a good work history at Food Fair Markets and Water Sports Distributing Company, as well as a lot of experience before that doing yard maintenance in my neighborhood. I don't know anything about photography but I'm a quick learner and I get along with other people very well. I know I can sell those high-end cameras and give your customers the best service they've ever had.

Boy, it sure is hard on your back standing up all day long behind this sales counter. Guess I'll get used to that in a little while. The bigger problem right now, though, is learning about photography and how to use all these high-end cameras and accessories. Makes you feel like an absolute idiot when customers ask you questions and you don't have any idea what they're talking about.

So tell me if I've got this right, Ed. The aperture and the shutter speed work together to allow the correct amount of light into the camera to expose the film. Reflex cameras give the most accurate view of the subject because you're looking right through the camera's lens. The depth of field is a function of the aperture; smaller aperture settings result in a greater depth of focus. The ASA number is an indication of the film's sensitivity to light; higher ASA film can be used to take pictures in low light conditions without flash. Developing your own black-and-white film is a three-step process: developer, stop bath, and water rinse.

You know, learning the basic principles of photography isn't all that difficult; in fact, it's quite interesting. But remembering all of the different features that each one of these high-end cameras and projectors has is difficult and time consuming. When you pick up that five-hundred-dollar Nikon camera and show it to a customer, you better know how that optional motorized back attaches and where the release button for the bayonet-mounted lens is located. Start fumbling around and you not only feel like an idiot but have no chance of making the sale.

So you have to spend every available minute going over all of that equipment so that you understand every detail. Can't figure it out? Get out the instruction book. Don't know why they make these things so hard to read and understand. All they really had to do was tell you to rotate that knob to the right before you tried to slide that switch to the left, but noooooo, that would be too simple.

Sure was funny when a customer came into the store with a torn roll of film stuck in his camera. That sort of thing happened often enough and was easy enough to fix if you knew what you were doing. Simply put the camera in that black cloth bag so that the light wouldn't spoil the film, insert your arms into the bag, open the camera, remove the film, and roll it back into its canister. Nothing to it, right? I'll give it a try.

Trouble was you had to know what you were doing. With only a few weeks on the job I didn't even know how to get the camera back open, so after trying for an endless period of time, I finally blurted out to the customer that I wouldn't be having trouble like this if he didn't have such an unusual camera. To which he responded that his camera was an Argus C3, the single highest-volume 35mm camera ever sold, up to that time. If both my arms hadn't been deeply stuck in that black changing bag I could have covered my face until the customer had left the store, but no such luck.

One of the unexpected benefits of working at Dunn's was that I found out that there really was a god, and this is how it happened: Dunn's had four stores in the suburban Detroit area. I had been hired to work at the Royal Oak store, so that's where I was supposed to spend most of my time. Shortly after I started, however, I was asked to temporarily fill in at our Northland store, so off I went. The manager, Bob, was a nice guy and he made me feel right at home when I showed up at his store one afternoon.

Bob knew that I was new and inexperienced, so he offered to show me how to work several of the movie projectors when there was a temporary lull in customer traffic. After setting up one of the projectors, Bob proceeded to take a roll of film that he used for customer demos and load it into the projector. Now we were ready to project the film onto a small screen so that he could show me how to run the projector.

All was going well as Bob turned on the projector and we began to watch the movie. To my surprise, the film was a home movie of a mother and her daughter playing outside on a swing set. Nothing wrong with that except the mother was unattractive and the daughter just wasn't a cute kid.

It made no sense at all to me to have a customer demo film that had absolutely no appeal. Why not show a bunch of cute girls having a picnic, or terrifying animals at a zoo? At least that would get the customer's attention. So after watching the movie for several minutes I was ready to blurt out, "Why do we have a demo film that features this dumpy woman?" At the exact instant that I was about to speak, Bob said, "This is my wife and daughter playing in the back yard of our house."

One quarter of a second? One half second at the most. That's all the time that separated Bob's comment from me opening my big mouth. I had witnessed a miracle; god had reached down and put his hand over my mouth just in the nick of time. Is there a god watching over us? Let me tell you with certainty: YES!

Dunn's was a great place to work for lots of reasons. The employees, the management, the owner, and the customers were usually a pleasure to be around. And Rochelle was one really hot number. Once I got familiar with the principles of photography, and all of the equipment, I frequently had higher sales commissions than anyone in the company's four stores. Friendly and courteous customer service always made the difference. Got a question about your camera? I'd give you a complete course in photography right there at the sales counter if you wanted it.

And customers wouldn't forget what you had done for them. Six months or a year later when they needed that special graduation gift, who do you think they asked for? Not good old Ed, the senior salesman and in-house photography expert who had theretofore been the unchallenged sales leader. Nope, they wanted to talk to that young guy who had taken the time to help them understand their camera last summer.

Every once in a while, though, a customer came in who was a real jerk. I remember once working the day before Christmas at our Birmingham store. Customers were ten deep at the sales counter and we were all going nuts just trying to keep up. A very haughty individual was standing in front of me asking all kinds of questions about his camera. I took the time, as I always did, to patiently explain everything to him even though he was condescending. That sort of thing happened occasionally because Birmingham was an upscale and affluent community, and some of its citizens thought they were better than everyone else. Over my shoulder I could see all the other sales personnel ringing up high-commission sales for expensive cameras and equipment, but I was still stuck with this guy who wasn't giving me any respect.

After selling him a roll of film, I thought I was finally finished with him, but I was wrong. He then asked me what the ASA number was on the film so I opened the film box, took out the instruction sheet, pointed to the highlighted number, and said the ASA is 25, it's shown here on this sheet. I wanted him to know that if he were to forget the ASA number later, it was printed on the sheet. Well, for some reason he didn't like that so he said in

a disgusted voice, "If I wanted to search for the ASA number I wouldn't have come into your store." In a flash I exploded, crumpled the paper into a ball, reached back and threw it as hard as I could right at his scowling face. A direct hit; bounced right off his nose. "Here, you look like you've got a third grade education, read it for yourself." I think I held my breath for at least a month after that incident but apparently nothing was ever reported to my boss; I kept my job.

Okay, this is the last month that I'll be working here at Dunn's. I've given Mr. Dunn my resignation letter and told him how much I appreciated having had the chance to work for him the past few years. He always knew that I'd be leaving once I started my co-op work assignment at the university, so my resignation came as no surprise to him. What came as a surprise to me, however, was what he wrote in a letter back to me. I've kept that letter all these years and always thought that it was the nicest thing anyone could have said to me: "…and if I had ever had a son, Mike, I would have been very pleased if he had turned out just like you."

Chapter 6
First Love

The affair has lasted nearly a lifetime with no signs of abatement. It began at an early age and now, as I creep up on old age, that first love still sits at the top of my list of needs and wants. She's always been an enabler; sometimes fast and furious, sometimes a thing of beauty, sometimes unreliable, always needy. Never once have we been separated, and I am certain that we'll be together until the very end. I wouldn't, I couldn't, I won't live without her.

She looks a little different now than she did many years ago, but she's every bit as beautiful. In 1955 she would pass by the corner where I was a "safety boy" every morning. She was gorgeous: long, low, shiny, red, and topless. Her name was Eldorado, and I wanted her more than anything else in the world.

In 1961 my boss at the time brought another beauty to work and I fell in love all over again. She looked a lot different then, mostly because of her beige color, but she was still gorgeous, powerful, and topless. He called her Bonneville. Here, try her out, he said.

I had gotten one of my own in 1960, two months before my sixteenth birthday. No, she wasn't anything like the perfect specimens that some others had because she was quite a bit older. Since 1953 she had been with others, there was no denying that. And she had kind of a funny name, Bel Air. But she was mine, she was black, she was topless, and I loved her dearly. No prejudice of any kind on my part! But I couldn't take her out until I turned sixteen; something about needing to have a driver's license. Didn't make any sense to me at the time, and it still doesn't. But the rules are the rules and when you're not the man in charge you've got to play by someone else's rules.

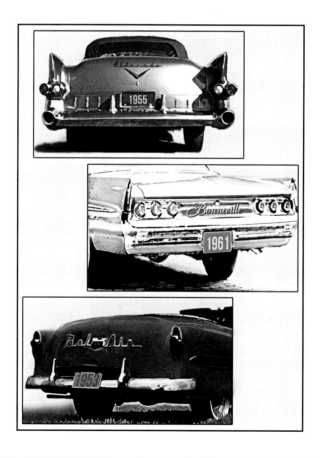

I had had to wait sixteen years and one day to get that license. Every day of that long wait was a struggle. And wouldn't you know it, my sixteenth birthday fell on a Sunday so I would have to wait one more day to take the exam to get my license. Go ahead, if you don't believe it, look it up: August 21, 1960, was a Sunday. Guaranteed. Rest assured that I was standing in line at the police station fifteen minutes before they opened that Monday morning. Come on, let's get this thing over with; my whole life has been on hold waiting for this thing.

But taking that exam turned out to be the easiest part of that ordeal. Getting the driver's training course that was a prerequisite for obtaining a license turned out to be almost impossible. The waiting list for the classes that were being given near my home was two years long. No way around it, either; simply not negotiable. Only the city of Detroit had immediate openings, but I didn't live in Detroit, so I had to find another way. But how?

Turns out that at the time I was attending St. Benedicts school in Highland Park, a city that just happened to be located within the geographic boundaries of Detroit. I started wondering if I could somehow convince the Detroit school district that I was then living in the city limits with my grandmother who had a home in Detroit. Grandma went along with the plan and through a stroke of luck I was able to pull off the deception. But at the time, the only driver's training session that was open in the entire Detroit district was deep in the heart of the city and about as far away from my home in Royal Oak as it could possibly be. But I had no choice; I took it.

I was already going to school far from my home in Royal Oak. But somehow I would have to find a way to get from my school to the remotest corner of Detroit in time for class and then find my way back home with no reliable means of transportation. What a job. The only way I had to get around was to hitchhike, and that's what I did. And since I was hitching a ride I sometimes had to guess if the driver's route was going to take me anywhere near where I needed to go. More than once I got stranded in some remote Detroit location because I didn't know my way around very well. But it was worth all of the aggravation. I would have done it had it taken ten times the effort.

But living with that first beauty of mine would always be difficult. She was temperamental, sometimes leaving me stranded in the middle of nowhere. And when she failed me I had no one to turn to and no money to pay for help.

Sure do wish I could have turned to Dad for some fatherly advice because it was all new to me. But Dad didn't really know anything more about her than I did. So when she acted up, as she often did, I had to resolve the problem all by myself.

She's making some really funny noises? Let's try this, or this, or this.

Damn it, Gordy, I just don't know what's wrong. How can we be lying on our backs for two weeks like this in the freezing cold and still not be able to figure this out?

Hard to believe that *that* was really all we needed to do.

Another learning experience!

New Year's Eve 1960 and we've got enough beer to turn this into the best time ever. But I've never seen the roads so slick; everything's covered with a sheet of ice. I know, I know that I'm weaving all over the place, guys, but it's the ice, not the beer. Okay, one of you guys take over while I get some sleep. Just be careful, I don't want to bang her up. Watch out, the road's turning and we're going straight. Crunch, smash…shit! Didn't know that he was worse off than I was.

Don't know how to fix her and don't have the money to have someone else do it. Guess I'll have to leave her the way she is. Actually, if you look at her from the other side she doesn't look quite as bad. But it really, really hurts deep down inside.

But I knew the day would come when I would have to find another. You know just as well as I do that most relationships don't last forever. So the search would begin for another beauty and it would repeat itself over and over again for a lifetime. In fact it was really no secret that I sometimes had more than one of those beauties at the same time. Don't act so surprised; lots of people have done the same thing.

Chapter 7
Oh Nooo!

Tap, tap, tap, tap, just keep doing it like I'm doing it. But whatever you do, don't break the skin. Keep rotating it and tapping it in different spots, but fairly gently. Then pass it to the guy behind you and tell him to do the same thing. After a couple of hours of gently tapping, that apple will be like a bag of applesauce. Then we'll put it on Sister's desk when she leaves the room for some reason. You know the nuns here at St. Benedicts feel like they can't throw any food away. Guess they think it's god's way or something. She'll feel obligated to eat it. Ha, ha, ha…

I can't believe that Johnnie's going to do that; man, that guy's got balls. Toss, miss; toss, miss; toss…he got it! That big rubber spider with a string around it is hanging from the light fixture right over Sister's desk. He's pulled it up so that it's more or less out of sight, up close to the light, and now he's pulled the string to the back of the room where he's going to sit. Since next class is study hall, Sister will be sitting at her desk for the whole hour.

Lower, lower, lower, lower…what a laugh riot. Sister has no idea what's going on: Why in the hell was her class erupting in laughter? Now higher, now lower again. Just how close to her was he going to get? Man, that guy's got balls. You've just got to envy that.

I'm not looking forward to the Latin test that's coming up next hour. Why in the hell do I need to know that stuff anyway? Sure wish there was some way to get out of it, but that ain't gonna happen.

Right behind that big closet door, behind Sister's desk, in the front of the room. That's where she keeps the test books locked up until it's time for the test. She'll pass them out, collect them, grade them, and then lock them back in the closet until the next test comes around. She'll be back in the room in a few minutes to pass out the test books. Crap!

Wait a minute, Larry's got a screwdriver in his hands, and he's walking up to the closet. What's he doing? He's loosening the set screw in the closet door handle and taking off the handle. Now he's pushed the handle stem inward so that the rest of the handle falls into the locked closet. What a great idea: can't get the locked closet door open without a handle, can you? Looks like no Latin test today, boys and girls.

Ha, ha, ha…no, Sister, don't know what could have happened to that door handle.

Oh man, she's in tears: "You're such bad children. I don't know what to do with you."

Aaaaachooooo!!!!!!! Oh my god, where in the hell did that come from? I've never sneezed like that in all my life. And right during the middle of study hall. I'm sure Sister is going to think that I did that intentionally, but I didn't. Honest!

No, Sister, that sneeze was real; I wasn't trying to disrupt study hall, honest. No, it was uncontrollable; it just came out unexpectedly. I didn't do anything…why are you sending me home? Nothing worse than being falsely accused. I'm innocent!

Well, yeah, maybe I did do a lot of those other things, but I didn't do anything this time. Maybe my reputation isn't so good.

So, brother Gordy, I'm a little surprised that Sister Rita's already got it in for you. First day of class and you haven't done anything wrong. So you say she was taking the class roll on the first day of the school year, and when she got to your name she repeated it twice and asked if you were my brother. Then she said she was going to keep a sharp eye on you because she didn't want another troublemaker in her class? *Oh nooo!*

Was about to turn sixteen and I had just purchased my first car, a 1953 Chevrolet convertible. Cost me $325, which was a huge amount of money to me at the time, but it was worth every penny. Had to work really hard to earn that money. Of course the car was anything but a perfect specimen, but I loved it dearly. No doubt about it, I was going to be pretty hot stuff when I showed that baby off to my friends.

Tenth grade at Cass Technical High School was all about cars. Who had the fastest, who had painted theirs candy-apple red, which make did the girls like best? Mine sure wasn't the fastest, and it wasn't painted some show-off color, but it was a convertible, and it was mine…not something that my parents were letting me borrow on occasion. Line up, girls, I'm open for business!

I couldn't wait to break the news to my buddies at school the next day. There I was, just after class started, waiting for a break in the lecture so I could tell my story.

Hey, Frank, guess what? I just bought a '53 Chevy convertible, and it's sitting in my driveway right now. I'll be off and running in a couple of months when I turn sixteen. (So whatd'ya think of that?)

What's that you say? Your parents just bought you a brand-new 390-cubic-inch, four-speed, hot rod 1960 Ford for your sixteenth birthday? Brand-new, you say? It was a gift? You didn't even have to pay for any of it? *Oh nooo!*

I'm going to need that money tomorrow, then, no more delays. I can't keep driving you and all the other guys back and forth to school like this without getting paid. Everyone else seems to come up with the money on time, but you're always late. Okay, tomorrow…but it's gotta be then.

Damn, these Michigan winters are cold; no way we can put the top down in weather like this. I know it's a long drive all the way to Cass Tech, guys, but just crowd a little closer together, we'll make it just fine.

Hey, we're really on a roll today; halfway there and we haven't caught a red light yet. No chance we're going to make it all the way without stopping, but it's fun to try. Speed up, slow down, just made that one. Hold on, boys, we're going to have to get some speed up to make this next one. These lights in Detroit are reasonably well timed, aren't they? Man, there's a chance to set the record if we can get through that last light just before school. No way; it's already turned red and we're about one hundred feet away. Looks like we're going to lose on the very last light…or are we? Hold on, boys, no traffic's coming the other way, I'm going through the red.

Made it all the way without stopping, even if we cheated on that last one. I'm calling it a new record; anyone disagree with me?

Sirens…red lights blazing away…they've got me, boys…I'm toast. The last thing I need is another ticket. No sir, I've never had a ticket before (or at least nothing in the last week or so). Any chance you can let me go on this one? No way, you say?

I wonder how long he's going to be back there writing up that ticket. Come on, asshole, we've got to get to school. What a prick; wouldn't even give me a break. I really hate jerks like that! Fuck 'em!

Bang, bang, bang, bang…shit, he's pounding on my window so hard he's going to break it. *Oh nooo!* He's been standing beside my door the whole time I've been mouthing off. He heard everything I said through the convertible top, even though my window has been closed. God, he's really pissed.

No sir, I didn't mean any of that. Bam, smack, stomp… stomp, smack, bam…this guy's going to kill me if he keeps this up much longer.

I'll drop you guys off at school but then I'm going back home to clean up and try to get it back together.

I didn't know how many tickets I could get before they took my driver's license away, but that possibility would have been an absolute disaster. I couldn't live my life without my car. But I'd been pulled over so many times, and I had gotten so many tickets. Good thing I had developed a special line of bullshit for every occasion. Talk your way out of it, that's the only way you could manage the problem. Don't even think about slowing down, or driving sanely. That's out of the question. Bullshit 'em, man; that's the only answer. Most of the time you could get away with it.

No sir, officer, I've never had a ticket before. I'm sorry about squealing those tires. If you give me a ticket my insurance rates will go up. You know I work hard to make enough money to support myself. I don't get anything from my parents. Thanks very much, sir; I won't do it again.

That might have worked about half the time. When it didn't, the only other thing you could do was to show up in traffic court and plead with the judge to dismiss the ticket. Surprising how often that approach worked.

Yes sir, your honor, I was speeding. But I'm a careful driver and if this ticket isn't dismissed my insurance rates will go up. You know I work hard to make enough money to support myself. I don't get anything from my parents. Thanks very much, sir; I won't do it again.

But the best thing that could happen if you did have to show up in traffic court was to find out that the cop wasn't there to press the charges. If they didn't show up for one reason or another, the judge was obligated to dismiss the ticket. Surprising how often that happened. Wasn't long before I started telling the cop at the time he issued the ticket that there was no way I could be in court to contest the ticket since I was always working or in school. Who knows how many times the cop remembered that and then decided not to show up in court. Whatever works; that's what I say!

Then there was the time that I had two tickets whose court dates were in consecutive weeks. Okay, okay, I'll just have to go through the same old bullshit twice.

At the first court appearance I was in extraordinarily good form. Case dismissed! So a few days later I had every reason to believe that history would repeat itself when I showed up again in court. But it turned out that the judge was the same guy I'd seen the week before. *Oh nooo!* What are the chances of that happening in a court system the size of Detroit's? Nothing else I could do but hope he wouldn't remember me.

Yes sir, your honor, I was speeding. But I'm a careful driver and if this ticket isn't dismissed my insurance rates will go up. You know I work hard to make enough money to support myself. I don't get anything from my parents.

"Weren't you here last week, son?" Yes sir, I was. "One to a customer. Get out of here!"

I had graduated from a '53 Chevy to an absolutely gorgeous '57 Oldsmobile, two-door hardtop, with the 371-cubic-inch tripower engine, floor-shifted manual transmission, and a midnight blue paint job. Every chance I got I was hot-rodding the thing. By the standards of the day it was a pretty fast car, so I had lots of street races under my belt. Over the course of a few years of abuse, I had replaced the manual transmission thirteen times and the clutch four times.

One time, after just having replaced the clutch and transmission, I hot-rodded away from the repair site and blew the transmission again. Hadn't gotten more than fifty feet before disaster struck. Damn!

Then there was the time I was stopped at a traffic light in Ferndale, Michigan, when a cop pulled up alongside me in his police car. He leaned out his window and asked, "Do you want to race that thing?" Oh man, this has got to be a trap. He wants me to hot-rod off so he can give me a ticket. I'm not falling for that one. Don't say anything to him. Just look straight ahead. When the light changes, take it easy.

When the light turned green the cop took off like a bat out of hell. He was laughing his ass off as he looked over his shoulder at me. Obviously, he thought he had won the race but I wasn't even racing. He was really hauling ass while he was looking back at me and laughing. Watch where you're going: that's the first rule of driving. But that clown was looking at me and didn't see the parked car that was on the other side of the intersection, and right in front of him. *Oh nooo!*

Screech, swerve, spin, tire smoke, but no collision.

Chapter 8
Contributing to the Delinquency of a Minor

It didn't take long to figure out that there was no better place to pick up girls than the mixers that were put on by the numerous nursing schools in and around the Detroit area. The girls' colleges in the area weren't bad either, but let's face it, you just couldn't beat a girl who had been repeatedly exposed to anatomy as part of her everyday course work. And besides that, girls' college girls usually had an inflated opinion of themselves, not to mention the fact that they had some inner sense of timing that always seemed to say "not so fast, bud, we hardly know each other." But the girls from the nursing schools were always approachable; perhaps that was due to the fact that there just weren't any guys in their classes. Yeah, those were the good old days when nurse meant female…with no exceptions.

So my friends and I always made the rounds in a never-ending search for some gorgeous girl to take to Friday night's party. Watching your friends do a double take when you walked in with some knockout girl hanging on your arm made all the effort and aggravation worthwhile. Not that it happened all that often; no, those times were few and far between. But when you did connect, I mean really connect, you knew why you had tried so hard. That's what you lived for; that was the reward for a job well done. Yeah, Frank, I'll ask her; I'm sure she has at least one hot girlfriend who will go out with you. But you're going to owe me one, pal; a really big one. Just don't screw it up for me.

I usually took the quantitative approach to connecting at those mixers, that is, the more phone numbers you got the better were your chances of connecting. Three or four phone numbers, maybe more, were the norm rather than the exception. Frequently I had a difficult time remembering who was who when I started calling them the next week. Now was she the blond who said she liked to water ski or the one who held on so tight when we were slow dancing? Think, man, think; you've got to have something to say when she picks up the phone. So you're busy that night, and those other two nights too, eh? Oh man, those rejections are painful, but you've got to hang in there. Hi, Sharon, this is Mike, I met you at the dance last Friday night…you said you like to water ski…Mike, about six foot one…

Yes, the quantitative approach always seemed to be the best answer. Just like in the lottery; the more tickets you buy, the better the chances are that you'll hit the jackpot. So in all things, great and small, that seemed to be the best approach. That sure was the case when I hit upon one of the best ideas of my life. As social chairman of the engineering fraternity that I belonged to, it was my job to set up parties of every type imaginable. One day I decided to set up a "blind date party," which meant that it was up to me to find blind dates for everyone in the fraternity. To do that I made up a two-page questionnaire that I dropped off at every nursing school and girls' college in the area. The questionnaire asked all kinds of personal and leading questions in the funniest way that I knew how to phrase them. And ended with the question: Would you like to go on a blind date with an engineer from our fraternity?

Well, the response was phenomenal, and I soon found myself in possession of a treasure chest of girls' names, phone numbers, measurements, and other vital statistics, and answers to some of the most important questions that can be asked: Are you the romantic type? Do you like to kiss on the first date? How far do you like to go; how far after that? You know you can't put a value on information like that! And I was the sole keeper of the vault, which meant that I was first in line, that I had every legitimate reason to call these girls, and that it was going to be a very good year. Night after night, thumbing through the responses. This one's got some smart-ass answers; I like that. Hello, is this Susan? Hi, Susan, this is Mike from Theta Tau fraternity. Do you remember the questionnaire that you filled out a couple of weeks ago? Well, it's my job here at the fraternity to double-check all of these for accuracy, so I thought I'd stop by tomorrow night to see if you were truthful. How about 7:00 p.m.?

Truthful? Sometimes but not always. It sure has been great meeting you; wish I had more time tonight but I've got a test tomorrow morning in thermodynamics. I had better get you back to the dorm; I'll call you…Then there was the one who immediately started bitching about everything that had gone wrong that day, and the day before that, and before that, on and on, on and on. By the time we got in the car, and then to the end of the block, I couldn't take it anymore, so I put the car in reverse and backed up all the way to the dorm, and then asked her to get out. Or the time I had a date with the close friend of the girl that I had seen the night before. She just happened to be the next person I called; how was I to know? And what were the chances that last night's date would end up walking through the lobby at the exact moment I was picking up her girlfriend? I'm trying to remember what I said at that fateful moment.

Good old Theta Tau; sure did have some good times then. Like when one of the guys had a great fund-raising idea. Why don't we put on a Computer Dance? We can use the computer to match everyone up according to how they fill out a questionnaire. (Another questionnaire?) We'll make a ton of money to help pay for our parties. It's a can't-miss. All we have to do is put together a computer program that will match everyone up automatically and then hire a band. What could be simpler than that?

And he was right. The Computer Dance became the rage on campus. We had so many participants that we couldn't fit them all into the student union. But the great part was that the Computer Dance provided me with another opportunity to take advantage of the system. Fraternity members were needed to accept the questionnaires that were returned when students bought tickets to the dance and I was more than happy to volunteer. Why wouldn't I volunteer? What better place for a person who wanted the pick of the litter? Throngs of students lined up buying tickets, half of them girls! Let's see, your name is Kathy? Hi, Kathy, thanks for buying a ticket to the dance; you know the computer will hook you up with someone who will be a perfect match. (And somehow I think that person is me. Let's just tuck Kathy's questionnaire right here in my pocket. No sense taking a chance that the computer might get it wrong, is there?)

Kathy and I had a great time at the dance, and at many fraternity parties that followed, too. When she ran for homecoming queen I was right there helping with the campaign. She didn't win but it was fun. Wonder how I missed the questionnaire that was turned in by the eventual winner. Oh, and I almost forgot. We could never get the computer program to work, so at the last minute we randomly matched everyone up. No one ever knew what happened but some of the matchups sure looked funny.

It all takes me back to those earlier days when I absolutely fell in love with Ruth at St. Benedicts school. It was seventh grade and I had just transferred to this awful school that was far away from my home, just because my mother thought I would get a better education at a parochial school. Anyway, at age twelve I had met the most beautiful, the smartest, the most interesting, and the sexiest girl in all the world. No one else came close. But, of course, there would never be any way of letting her know how I felt or of knowing if she had any feelings for me. That sort of thing was unfathomable for a kid who still wasn't even sure what the other

kids meant when they said that they had been "making out" with some girl the night before.

Then an amazing thing happened. Several of us were staying after school for one lame reason or another. As I sat there trying to finish my work, I was watching Ruth out of the corner of my eye and listening to every word she was saying to one of her girlfriends. Such beauty, such poetry. Then, from out of nowhere, another girl in the class came up and handed me a neatly folded handwritten note: *Did you know that Ruth really likes you?* There is truly something special that happens when a "first" of any kind is experienced. What words can describe that feeling? The first game-winning home run that you hit. The first time you take something apart and then are able to put it back together again successfully. They're all confidence builders but nothing would ever again elevate me higher than finding out that *Ruth really likes you.*

But it was anything but smooth sailing from that point on. Up, then down. Left, right; man, this ride is making me dizzy.

Evelyn was a real piece of work. We had been "going steady," I guess that's what we called it then, for something like twelve months, and she wanted to get married. Get married? At age sixteen? Are you nuts? (I'm sure I said it more diplomatically than that.) But it all came to a crashing end the day we were at the beach and she began flirting with some other guy. Are you kidding me? What in the hell was that all about? What do you mean I wasn't paying enough attention to you? Go see if he'll give you a ride home; I'm leaving! I guess her father had every right to be really pissed off at me, leaving his daughter about forty miles from home like that. But she had it coming.

And then there was the time that Carolina wanted to watch the submarine races at the Detroit River. Actually, it's almost too embarrassing to talk about, but I'll mention it anyway. Stupid, the last thing you ever want a girl to think is that you're stupid. And when you combine stupid with novice you get a combination that is doomed to failure. Submarine races? They don't race submarines on the river, and if they did it sure wouldn't be at this time of night...so now you want to go home just because I don't want to watch submarines racing?

One of the funniest things that ever happened to me took place when I was seventeen. It was Friday and I had a date with a girl I hadn't known very long. All was right with the world up until the phone rang with the bad news; she wasn't going to be

able to go out that night. But, she said, she had a girlfriend who wanted to go out with me in her place. Since I didn't have any better options, I said that would be fine. However, there was one minor issue. Her girlfriend was eighteen, one year older than me, and she wouldn't want to go out with anyone younger than herself. No big deal, I'll just tell her that I'm eighteen. It wouldn't be the first time I had lied about my age. Actually, she turned out to be really cute and we hit it off right away. So after spending a couple of hours at a party, we decided that we would have more fun somewhere where we could be alone so that we could finish off the rather large supply of beer that I had in the trunk of my car. So there we were, parked on a deserted cul-de-sac, feeling the full effects of the beer and having a great time. Trouble was that we were throwing the beer bottles out the window, just so that we could hear them break against the pavement. Don't ask me why we did that, we just did.

After a couple of hours, the inevitable happened; the cops showed up and hauled both of us off to the county jail. While they were processing the two of us, they asked our ages. Eighteen, she said; eighteen, I said. And so we were both booked and then taken away to jail cells where we were to stay until our Monday-morning court appearance. All I remembered from that night was the absolutely filthy grease-covered army blanket that was thrown over the cold springs of the bunk bed that protruded from the wall.

Along about 6:00 the next evening, I had had about all I wanted of the Oakland County Jail. It was then that I happened to mention to one of the other inmates that I was seventeen but I had told the police officers that I was eighteen to protect my cover with my date. They can't keep you in jail if you're only seventeen, man. You've got to tell them; they'll have to let you out. Sure enough, several hours later I was home listening to the ranting and raving of my old man. I'd never seen him so mad. No one had known if I was alive or dead, since I hadn't even been allowed to make a phone call the night before.

Well, that's not the end of the story. When the court found out that I was underage, they charged my female partner in crime with contributing to the delinquency of a minor. Can you believe

that? The indignity of it all! I knew it was all a big misunderstand-
ing and I hoped that all would be forgiven. But for some reason she
wouldn't go out with me again; she wouldn't even talk to me...and
we had gotten along so well.

Chapter 9

Once Upon a Time

Nursing schools in the Detroit area had mixers all through the school year, so there was almost never a week without something going on. And in those days almost the entire student body at nursing schools was female, which meant the everyday classroom setting didn't provide much opportunity for these nurses to meet guys. Too bad for them; great for those of us who wanted to meet girls and who liked to dance.

It was Tuesday, January 10, 1967. Providence Nursing School had scheduled a mixer and my friend and I showed up. It was one of those typically cold Michigan winters, so when we walked into the building the first thing we did was go to the coat check area to drop off our things. That turned out to be a good move because one of the girls behind the counter was absolutely gorgeous. Not just cute, she was drop-dead gorgeous. Suddenly at a loss for words, which was not at all unusual, the only thing I could think to say was, "Do you have to stay here all night or can you come out and dance?" Not poetic, not witty, not clever, just unimaginative, dry, dull. I'd have to do better than that if I was going to get her interested in me.

And it only got worse. I don't think she had any intention of taking me up on my offer to dance, but when she eventually did show up at the dance floor I was there in a flash. Can't remember what I said next but I do know that everything that came out of my mouth sounded idiotic. If she hadn't been such a doll the whole thing would have been a lot easier to pull off. But you know how it goes, when you really, really want something, the chances of screwing it up increase proportionately. And I was on a downward spiral. The more pressure I put on myself, the worse it got.

If she had followed her instincts she would have told me to shove off, but she didn't. Maybe she just felt sorry for me. Whatever it was, I hung around all night and continued to engage her in uninspired conversation. At one point I asked how old she was. Eighteen, she answered. I was twenty-two, and eighteen seemed young to me, so I proceeded to make a big deal out of the whole thing. Who knows why; it was all part of the out-of-control spiral that I was in. When the evening finally drew to an end I was surprised when she gave me her phone number and agreed to go out with me. I've still got that scrap of paper she wrote her number on.

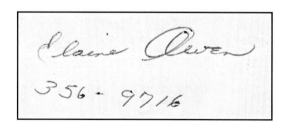

So we made a date to go to a fraternity party that I, as social chairman, was responsible for setting up. I had always brought sharp girls to our parties, but this time I was bringing someone who would leave the other guys speechless. No, I didn't need to say a thing; when I walked in with this girl on my arm I would prove once again that they had all been right when they gave me the fraternity's Best Mover award. I couldn't wait to see the look on their faces; I would be smug and as nonchalant as always. "Oh hi, guys, say hello to Elaine."

But I had an uncomfortable feeling that Friday before the party. What if she had changed her mind? That wouldn't have surprised me at all, since I felt things had initially gotten off to such a bad start. In an interesting turn of events, one of the guys I was living with was looking for a date that night, so I thought I'd call Elaine to see if she had a friend for him. More importantly, that gave me a reason to call so that I could size up the situation. The phone conversation wasn't at all reassuring; it seemed like I was heading for a last-minute rejection, so I tried to preempt that possibility by saying something along the lines of, "You're not going to tell me you can't go tonight, are you?" Her quick response was, "No, I wasn't about to say that." In fact, she told me later that she was going to say that very thing but I had taken her by surprise and she didn't know what to say.

Funny how things go, isn't it? A few words said differently or a slight change in timing, and life would have been altogether different in so many ways. No Matthew, no Alex, no Dan, no Kristina. All the good times that followed, all the hard times that followed…

never to have been. A different word, a split-second difference in timing, that's all it would have taken. What would life have been like without her?

But we did go to the party and we did have a good time, even though she later said that she thought I would try to get her drunk that night for ill-begotten reasons. On that charge I am innocent. She later confessed that she had a fear of going to a party with a bunch of misbehaving fraternity guys, and that that had been the biggest issue that night.

But forward we went from there.

A few dates later I would pick her up at her home for the first time, instead of at her dorm. Man, that was an experience. When I walked in the door, her parents were in the middle of a major verbal confrontation and my presence did absolutely nothing to change things. I couldn't believe what I was hearing nor could I believe they didn't stop when I arrived. But on and on they went, just like I wasn't even there. It was evident that her father was dead drunk and that her mother could yell and carry on with the best of them. The arguing part I was used to from my own home experiences, but I was certain that my parents would have shut up in the presence of a guest. But that wasn't to be. As we walked out the door, I didn't know what to think.

But I did know that that kind of thing was never going to happen to me. I was certain that I could manage things so much better than that. I was confident that I could succeed where others had failed. So, little did I fear that the product of two stressful home environments could produce a carbon copy of itself. Confidence is usually a good thing, but there are times when it can act as a set of blinders. The life that Elaine and I were to embark on together would vary between polar extremes until it finally came to an end after twenty-seven years.

There we were, supremely confident and ready to take on the world. We were going to show them all how it was supposed to be done. With my newly minted engineering degree in my hand, the keys to my 1965 Chevelle in my pocket, and enough money in my wallet to buy lunch, we began our journey.

We had a total of forty dollars to furnish our first apartment, so it was obvious that we were going to have to make do with the discards offered by family and friends. Mom's old paisley studio couch sat in the living room. Our dining room suite was a folding card table and chairs that had been a recent gift from a family member. As I

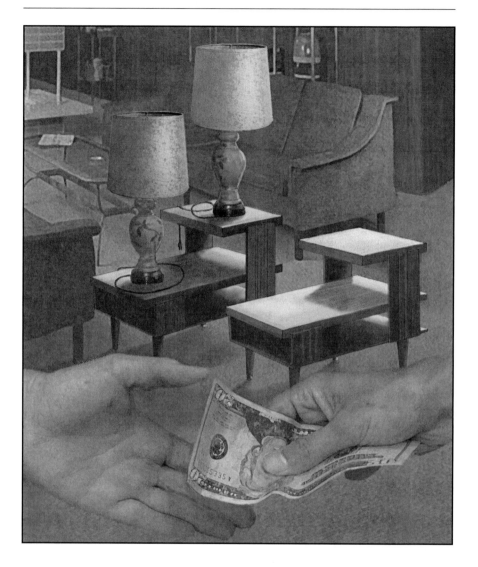

remember it, that was the only new thing that we had in the entire apartment. We didn't have a bed or a box spring, so a three-quarter-size mattress on the floor had to do. The kitchen was equipped with a collection of plates, glasses, pots and pans, knives and forks, and other miscellaneous castoffs from every corner of the earth. And twenty of the forty dollars that we had to spend went to buy two used blond end tables with matching lamps, at a cost of five dollars each. When I brought them home, Elaine said the end tables were ugly; to me they weren't all that bad, except for the blond color. Can't remember where we spent the remaining twenty dollars.

Newly married with no kids; life should have been nothing but fun and laughter. But the graduate work that I was doing concurrent with my employment added an enormous burden to our lives. So we weren't out sailing with our friends on the weekends or jumping on a plane to see the sights in New York City. That would have to come later. We were working to build our future. If *we* didn't do it, who would do it for us? No rich relatives, no one to show the way, or to grease the skids. But fuck 'em all, given a little more time we knew we'd kick all their asses…which we did.

Not sure how it happened; maybe "the pill" had been forgotten. But you guessed it, soon there would be three of us. No, we hadn't expected it quite yet, but something great was about to happen and we were excited. When Elaine came home from work the next day she was greeted by flowers throughout the apartment.

We had moved into our first home in Royal Oak, Michigan, with one child in hand and another on the way. It was a small home, in good condition, and in a nice neighborhood. It's true that the exterior paint was peeling in some places, but that was to be expected in a wood-sided home. It took a while, but we repaid every penny of the ten-thousand-dollar equity loan that we got from a business acquaintance of my mother. Without that loan we never would have been able to qualify for the mortgage from the bank.

It wasn't long before we had the place fixed up and looking good. At the time, we thought the red plastic stick-on brick that we put on one wall in the room we prepared for Matt, our first-born, was slick. For Alex, our second oldest, we had giant cartoon animals on the walls. The blond end tables were still in the living room, along with the paisley studio couch, but we actually had a bed and a box spring in our bedroom. Seems like we also had added a dresser so that we no longer had to keep our things in piles around the perimeter of our bedroom.

We were learning how to raise kids, maintain a household, survive on a limited budget, and enjoy the relatively simple pleasures that life had to offer. With my graduate work finally behind me and my job going well, it still seemed like there was nothing we couldn't do and that nothing could stop us. But we were about to find out that our lives were in some ways just like the ones we had known as kids. That shouldn't have surprised us, but it did. Arguments, financial stresses, kids who acted like kids, and the fact that we were developing different needs and goals, all were about to surface.

The process of growing apart creeps up on you. Sometimes it is so difficult to see that you're not even sure it's there. Then the rewarding and fun experiences begin to be overshadowed by disagreements and disappointments. It didn't all turn bad and it didn't happen all at once. But change began to cloud the vision, and the ideals that I had carried around for a lifetime began to lose focus.

Looking back with the aid of time compression, it is easier to see, but in real time it's much more subtle.

So onward we sailed, paying little attention to the leaking boat that we were in. It seems obvious now that things might have been saved if we had spent more time early on addressing the problems. But we were moving forward at a high rate of speed and nothing could slow us down. Daniel, our third son, had arrived, and we had purchased a home in Farmington, Michigan. Repairing our leaking boat was the last thing on our minds at the time.

The Farmington home wasn't much bigger than the home we had just moved from, but it was all brick and it was in a somewhat upscale neighborhood. Our three boys were doing okay for the most part, but it was clear early on that none of them was going to fulfill their father's dream of being captain of the football team or the next senator from Michigan. Oh well, fame and glory hadn't been in the cards that he had been dealt as a kid either. But in spite of the great deal of time and effort that it took to raise them, and the worry and occasional heartache that seemed to occur at far too frequent intervals, they became the brightest part of our lives and our greatest hope for the future.

I've always regretted that our kids were exposed to the frequent conflicts that Elaine and I had. It had turned out to be just like the home life I had experienced, but fortunately not nearly as bad as what Elaine had gone through. We had full and active lives, so there were plenty of good times that went along with the bad. But even though the good may have outweighed the bad, might even have far outweighed the bad, the part that lingers is the conflict. Why is that?

By the late 1970s we had progressed to a far better place in terms of job and financial status, so it seemed like the time was right to build our first home. We chose Brighton, Michigan, a community that was relatively distant from the suburban Detroit area but had much to offer in terms of scenic beauty, good schools, and the general proximity of the University of Michigan, in Ann Arbor. Starting with a set of plans that were furnished by our builder, we set out to customize the home in a manner that suited us. Not a square foot of space was wasted. Hallways were minimized, closet space was optimized, and we were able to place the garage at basement level due to the hilly nature of the terrain. The end product turned out to be everything we had hoped for and more.

At the time we committed to building the home, I was still working at Eaton Corporation's Engineering and Research Center, which was a forty-minute drive from the Brighton home site. However, midway through the building process I took a job at Rockwell International, which was twenty minutes farther away. One of my reservations about the Rockwell job was the one-hour drive that I would have to make twice each day. Forty minutes to Eaton was already pushing it, but I went ahead anyway. I'm tempted to say that taking the Rockwell job was a big mistake, not just because of the driving time, but for countless other reasons as well. But then again, if I had not gone down that path the good things that followed later in my career wouldn't have happened as they did, either.

That drive took so much time out of my already long and busy day that I came to regret building a home so far from where the rest of my life was centered. Wasn't long before the stress and strain of all that had begun to take its toll on our family life. As always, there were plenty of good times. I know they were there, but I have always found them harder to remember. Why is that?

Then a telephone call came from a recruiter who told me about a vice president of engineering and quality assurance job at a company called Bristol Compressors, in Bristol, Virginia, located right at the Virginia-Tennessee state line. I had absolutely no interest in the job. But since I had never seen much of that part of the country, and since I had nothing planned for the upcoming weekend, I thought I'd take an all-expenses-paid holiday courtesy of Bristol Compressors. I had nothing better to do, and getting away from the job I hated for a few days sounded like fun. And who knows, maybe something unexpected would happen.

So off I went to interview for a job I had no intention of taking. But somehow, after several more visits, including visits with Elaine, I was looking at a job offer that sounded far more appealing than I had thought possible: good salary and bonus program, company car and country club membership, a small equity position in the company, a move package that included a cash incentive, and a limited non-termination contract. That was a far better deal than I had at Rockwell. But did I really want to leave everything and everyone I knew and move to some place I had never even heard of before the whole process started? Surely not! And did I mention that the people down there spoke kind of funny? "We would sure be pleased if you all would come down and join us."

Had Elaine not repeatedly encouraged me to make the move, it never would have happened. In fact, the only problem that I had was figuring out how to tell Rod, the president of Bristol, who was also one of the owners, that I was going to turn down the offer. Rod wanted me to come and he was a persuasive guy. When Rod called I just couldn't find the words or the courage to say no.

It was 1983. Off we went to Bristol. The two cars we were driving to Bristol were stuffed with all the things we couldn't load on the moving van, our three kids, one dog, and a cat. Then, at the end of a long day's drive, we encountered a minor disaster: when we finally got into the Bristol area late that night, we ended up mistakenly taking different exits, getting separated and completely lost. Since our home was in a somewhat rural area outside the city, we both felt like we were in some primitive land. It took each of us a long time to figure out where the other was. No cell phones in those days. Not a good start.

And the company itself was in poor financial shape. Sales were a fraction of the plant capacity, our product was not competitive from a design standpoint, and we were carrying a high debt load, to name just a few of the problems. In reality, the company wasn't all that far from closing its doors. If I had understood that better I would have had one more powerful reason for not taking the job.

You couldn't say that it was all part of some grand plan. Call it luck if you want; we're all entitled to a little of that, aren't we? Whatever. Turns out that taking the Bristol job was the best career move I ever made. We absolutely loved the Bristol area. The weather was great, the people were great, Rod and the board of directors were great, and Elaine was happy. About one year after joining Bristol, I got promoted to president and became a member of the board of directors. Several years later, our sales, profits, and employment had climbed to extraordinary levels. Two years after moving to Bristol, we started building a beautiful new home that was right across the street from the home we were living in. Life was good. And then York International showed up.

Actually, they had come to look us over at the invitation of our board of directors. The board's plan had always been to fix up the company and sell it, for the owners to make a lot of money, and for everyone to live happily ever after. It had taken four years to get Bristol to that point, but the whole transaction was over in a flash. We were now owned by York International, the largest independent heating, ventilating, air-conditioning, and refrigeration (HVAC&R) company in the world. I had received enough money from the sale of my small share of the company to feel fairly comfortable, so I was fine with the deal. York asked if I would continue as president of Bristol under their ownership, which I agreed to do.

Bristol continued to prosper under York's ownership, and one year after the sale I was asked by York's board of directors to take over as president of York, the parent company, and to join the board. This new position would require a move to York, Pennsylvania, something that neither Elaine nor I wanted to do. To complicate matters, the York board had told me when they offered me the job that they intended to put the company up for sale, which meant that in my new position I would have to deal with the uncertainty that comes with new ownership. Couldn't turn down the job as president of a Fortune 500 company, but it seemed best to wait to move the family until I saw how things turned out. I moved to York; Elaine and the kids stayed in Bristol.

Living alone in York, Pennsylvania, wasn't all bad. The demands on my time in my new position didn't leave much room for family life anyway. And, because of an agreement that I had with the board, I was able to use the company plane to fly back and forth to Bristol on the weekends. Whenever possible, I would tie the return to Bristol to a business-related trip to help justify the cost and time spent on those trips. The whole process was complicated and demanding, which came as no surprise. The challenge, however, came as a result of the uncertainty that accompanied the upcoming sale of the company. Would the new owners retain the management team or would they choose to replace it?

Elaine and I were being pulled in many different directions. We liked living in Tennessee; we weren't so sure about Pennsylvania. We had started building the new home in Tennessee prior to the York job offer. Did we want to abandon that? New housing in the York area was in short supply. Did we want to take what was available and make the best of it? And where would we be if the new owners of the company were difficult to work with or if they wanted to install their own management team? That sort of thing happened all the time.

The biggest complicating factor, however, was that I had never really wanted to spend my working life in someone else's employment. When I began my working career, I had every intention of starting my own business just as soon as I was able to do so. To this end, I had always worked on my own new product ideas, on my own time, and with my own money. I had every expectation that when I finally did hit on the right idea, I would start my own business. But it seemed that the time had never been right to make that leap. After all, the companies that I had worked for kept promoting me and compensating me at levels few others ever reached. It had always been difficult to cut the ties.

Whenever I found myself in the midst of uncertainty, I always tried to play all the hands at once. This time would be no different. I had moved to York and the family had stayed in Bristol. We continued building the home in Bristol and also bought a home that was under construction in York. I gave my new job everything I had while simultaneously thinking about going out on my own as soon as the company was sold. I was in Pennsylvania during the week and in Tennessee on most weekends. We decided to wait and see how things turned out with the pending sale of the company.

Following a slow and agonizing process, York was finally sold to Citicorp Venture Capital. I had been compensated well for my equity ownership in the company and I was financially secure. After taking control of York, Citicorp offered me an attractive package to stay on as president of the company. Their plan was to sell the company in a few years at a substantial profit and make everyone rich, including themselves. Most importantly themselves. The classic "leveraged buyout" process was in place, and the dice had been rolled.

The Citicorp deal was one that would be difficult to turn my back on. What was I going to do?

"To Citicorp and the York Board of Directors: After much thought and deliberation I have decided to resign my position as president and COO of York International to pursue my own personal business ventures. It is my intention to step down from my current position as soon as the board has identified and put in place my successor."

Yes, Jim, I've given it a great deal of thought. I appreciate that Citicorp and the board wish me to stay on, but this is a career step that I've wanted to take for a long time; I've got to move on now. Thanks again for all that you and the rest of the board have done for me.

Elaine, my stuff is packed, the York home is listed with a Realtor, and I'll be driving back to Bristol tomorrow.

I love driving with the top down on a beautiful spring day. Free at last, free at last, damn, I'm free at last. All the thoughts that are in my head right now. From the very day I turned sixteen I'd been tethered to the plow. Not one single day during those twenty-eight years had I been without a job. Not one. Even before age sixteen I always worked. And now my time was all my own. Going to get a good night's sleep and then fuck off tomorrow! Nineteen eighty-nine is going to be a very good year.

So did you really think that getting a new HVAC business started was going to be easy? Especially one that required so much capital. And you'd have to get the management team lined up and convince them all that they should walk away from their well-paying jobs and move their families to Bristol. And you had to hope that the business plan that you had put so much effort into would convince those wealthy potential investors to part with many tens of millions of dollars. And the local municipal government had to be convinced that you would bring jobs to the region if you were to secure land and start-up capital from them.

And while you're trying to set up a new HVAC company, why not take on a few side ventures? Like building a car wash, and building affordable housing? No, you wouldn't do those things just like everyone else. You always had a different slant on things that always gave you an advantage. And one more thing, why not make a financial investment in a venture that a business acquaintance of yours was starting up?

Sure had a lot going on. Was probably as busy as I had been when I worked for York. Elaine had been supportive, but working out of my home office had us in close proximity all the time. The new house was great, but why had we built it so big? And the kids were a handful. And at the last minute, Pete had decided that he didn't want to head up the new HVAC company that we'd been working so hard to start. Stress was building up and absolutely nothing was going right. Things started to look dark. I had all the symptoms of extreme depression, something I'd heard about but never fully appreciated. If you have never been there yourself, you could never understand!

Elaine said I needed to check into a hospital to get help, but I didn't know what they were going to do to help me. She was worried and insisted that I go. Okay!

What a mistake. I'd known my whole life that I could never, ever put myself in someone else's hands. Checking into the hospital meant losing control. I'd only been there for a couple of hours but I already knew that I had to do everything in my power to get out. Of course the doctor's main concern was that I was so depressed that I was going to commit suicide. So my job was to convince him that I was perfectly fine. The whole thing was just a brief bout of melancholy. All gone now…so let me out of this goddamn place! I was in an extreme state of depression but smiling and acting as if everything was great. That was hard to do but it was clear that that was what I had to do. Two days was all it took and I was home. Of course nothing had changed. But I had started taking Prozac.

Whoever it was who came up with that drug should be given a medal. Almost immediately I began to feel better, even though the drug was supposed to take several weeks to act. Not in my case. And of course the side effects were there too. Always seemed like if there was a side effect of any kind I'd find it. Inability to sleep, inability to fuck…that was the worst of it. So I battled my way through the mess and came out a few months later feeling great. Hadn't taken long but it sure had been tough.

Then in the early spring of 1991 I got a phone call from Beacon Capital, an investment firm located in Toronto, Canada. Beacon had heard about me from several different sources in the HVAC industry and wanted to know if I would consider joining them as a major equity partner in a business that they had purchased from the Coleman Company, in Wichita, Kansas. Coleman had spun off their HVAC operations about a year earlier, and the buyer, Beacon Capital, had been trying to make a go of it in the interim but things weren't going well. Would I consider joining them as an owner, chairman of the board, and CEO of this recent acquisition, which had been renamed Evcon Industries? They had to be kidding, right? Two years before I had walked away from York International, a Fortune 500 company that was over twenty times the size of Evcon. Why would I be interested in going to work at Evcon? But I was flattered, and Jack, the Beacon CEO, was very persuasive so I decided to take an all-expenses-paid trip to Toronto. But I was never going back to the industry in any way other than through my own company, or so I thought.

After several more discussions and several clandestine trips to Wichita, I was hooked. The offer that Beacon made was extraordinary, and I had not been successful in getting my own HVAC company started. Recall that Pete, the person who was supposed to run the HVAC company for me, had backed out at the last minute, and none of my other ventures were doing all that well either. Timing is everything. Beacon had called at precisely the right moment. What the hell, I thought, I think I'll give this a try.

Elaine was in disbelief. Why in the world would I consider heading up a company in Wichita, Kansas? Why had I left York

International, anyway? Was I nuts? To make things worse, she loved living in Bristol and didn't find anything at all she liked in Wichita. And things took a turn for the worse when I unilaterally decided that a small home in suburban Wichita would be ideal for us. It was immediately available, close to the school that Dan was going to attend, was in a beautiful subdivision, and was attractively priced. But the home was nowhere near the magnificent structure we had built in Bristol. She never got over the move. The difficulties that the two of us were having only got worse.

We finally sold the home in Bristol, which seemed to cut Elaine off from any thoughts that might have lingered about returning to our earlier life. And the first home in Wichita was soon gone, having been replaced by a much more elegant home that we subsequently completely remodeled. As kids we had both lived in modest homes, but that was now certainly out of the question. How things had changed.

Fortunately, the Evcon venture was going well. The Beacon Capital group had turned out to be great to work with, but of greater importance was that the complete transformation of the business we had embarked on was showing results. Sales and profits had skyrocketed. As with Bristol Compressors, the plan had always been to fix up the company and sell it. So when York International called one day to say they were interested in buying the business, we were neither surprised nor uninterested.

Wasn't that something? York International, the company that had once purchased Bristol Compressors, and that I had formerly headed up, was now interested in buying Evcon Industries. We went through some intense negotiation but in the end the deal was done. Ownership was to change hands near the end of 1995, at which time I retired for the second time. The financial windfall was enormous. Free again, free again, thank god I'm free again.

Free again in more than one way: Elaine and I had finally decided to end our marriage. But the process of splitting up was difficult. Just one more example of our inability ever to see eye to eye. She had a far better lawyer than I had, and there was no way they were going to make things easy. How unfortunate, because from the start I had expressed my willingness to split everything fifty-fifty and to give her first pick on all assets that weren't liquid. How could anything have been more straightforward than that?

That was symptomatic of the problem, however. I thought I was approaching things in a reasonable manner but, as we all know, most problems are the result of both parties' failure. I'm sure she has an equally valid, opposite point of view on the settlement as well as all of the other problems that we encountered over the years. I've always admitted to being at least 50 percent of the problem.

I've conveniently omitted many of my shortcomings from this story simply because they are far too painful to admit. Let your imagination go and you can guess at some of the things that were clearly my fault and that could never be reconciled.

The grief I felt when it was finally over is difficult to put into words. I needed to escape from the reality of the moment, but at the same time I needed to fully experience the sorrow that was so very real. So I searched my music collection for my all-time favorite recording, *Once Upon a Time* from the Broadway play *All American*, sung by Ray Bolger and Eileen Herlie. Over and over again I replayed the song while I was driving around aimlessly in my car. When the tape finally jammed, I was devastated but continued to scroll through the words in my mind:

Once upon a time, a girl with moonlight in her eyes, put her hand in mine and said she loved me so. But that was once upon a time, very long ago.

Once upon a hill, we sat beneath a willow tree, counting all the stars and waiting for the dawn. But that was once upon a time, now the tree is gone.

How the breeze ruffled through her hair. How we always laughed as though tomorrow wasn't there. We were young and didn't have a care. Where did it go?

Once upon a time, the world was sweeter than we knew. Everything was ours, how happy we were then. But somehow once upon a time never comes again.

Once upon a time, it seemed the world was painted gold, and there was a man and, oh, I loved him so. The world was beautiful to see, very long ago.

On a night like this, we saw the rising of the moon. All the silver stars like necklaces were strung. We spoke of such important things. We were very young.

Open hearts, nothing to conceal, every little thought was so exciting to reveal. All our dreams we knew would soon be real. Where did they go?

Once upon a time, the world was sweeter than we knew. Everything was ours, how happy we were then. But somehow once upon a time never comes again.

Chapter 10
Tell Me It's Finally Over

I was pretty sure that I'd be able to take any one of them if it turned out to be a fair fight. Maybe not always in fisticuffs because I didn't necessarily have a distinct advantage there. But when it came to a heads-up competition in the business world I knew that I'd be able to outthink 'em and outwork 'em every time. But what if it wasn't a fair fight? What if their family owned the company? Or what if they got ahead of me just because they had better educational credentials? That wouldn't be good at all. Figured there wasn't anything I could do about the family business situation, but the educational part I could do something about. But god, I hated going to school. I'd hated it from first grade. And now, all these years later, I was sitting in a classroom in the second year of engineering school realizing that I had a lot more than three years to go before I would finish up this educational stuff.

So, Dean Canjar, tell me more about this doctoral program here at the University of Detroit. Sixty-some hours after the bachelor's, written and oral exams prior to admission, work in industry to solve a real-world highly technical problem, written proposal with oral presentation, and thesis followed by an oral defense. Can you say all that again, this time a little slower? You're not kidding, are you?

So let's think this thing through. They'll let me start taking graduate courses before I finish my bachelor's so that I can get a jump on things. I can take some of those classes during the co-op work semesters. Okay, that'll work. Finding a company that will allow me to work on a high-level problem that will satisfy their needs as well as the needs of the university won't be easy, but I'll figure that out somehow. Going to need a university adviser and a joint university-industry committee too. Who should I ask to be my adviser? Need someone who carries a lot of weight around the U; someone who can clear the path for me and put some of these idiotic professors in the engineering school in their place when that becomes necessary. Someone whom I really like a lot, too. Dean Canjar, I was wondering if you would consider…

These co-op assignments at Cadillac Gage are really great. Learning a lot about hydraulics and servo-mechanism control systems. This is challenging and high-level stuff; can't imagine being at a place like Ford Motor Company where I might be working on door locks or the like. How could anyone end up doing something like that, anyway?

I'm so tired, though, working all day and going to school and studying all night. Got to think of a way to get some of this studying done while I'm here at work, but how? What if I came in to work about thirty minutes early and Xeroxed the pages out of my textbooks; then I could punch them with three holes and put them in a loose-leaf binder along with company work-related pages. See, this page is company, this page is school; company, school, company, school. Hold the binder partly open to the school page with your finger in front of the preceding company page; let the page fall when someone approaches your desk …Oh, hi, Bob, how's the testing going on the stabilization system for the M60A1E1 tank gun?

Got another idea, too. That army armored personnel carrier that's sitting in the far corner of the test garage doesn't have any windows in the back portion where the troops are carried. Those long bench seats in the back look awfully good; a person could stretch right out and take a quick nap if he was really, really tired, couldn't he? And if he brought a lot of test equipment in with him and laid it there, there, and over there, then it would look like he was working if someone unexpectedly opened that massive rear door. In fact, you could be sound asleep in there and instantly wake up in the time it would take someone to open that huge door. Worth a try if you're so tired that you can't keep your eyes open… clunk, squeak, thud…what the fuck…where in the hell am I? Oh, hi, Mr. M, just getting some test data; I'll have that report on your desk first thing in the morning.

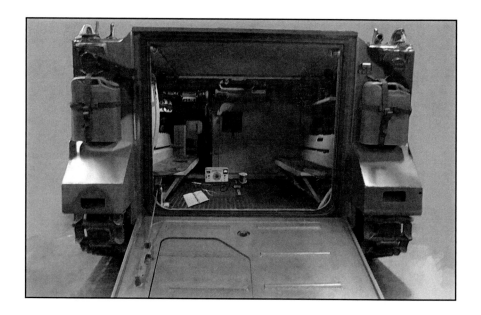

Someone really ought to write a research paper on sleep. Few people probably know the extreme momentary agony that the mind and body go through if they must suddenly awaken from a deep sleep and instantly sound lucid and responsive. Say in about two seconds, the time it takes to open a massive door.

The work here at Cadillac Gage is challenging, but employees are treated badly. I've had other jobs before, but I've never seen anything like this. The vice president of the engineering department never says hello when he passes you in the office; doesn't even look up, as a matter of fact. Anyway, it was just the other day when he stormed out of his office and came over to the guy who sits at the desk next to mine. In his loudest voice he berated and cursed the guy prior to firing him. Everyone heard it. You know, that's not the way I'm going to do things when I run a company.

That's part of the reason I couldn't understand why this guy Ed came back to work here at Cadillac Gage. Says he originally left the company to join the Eaton Engineering and Research Center on the other side of town. Says he left the job at Eaton because the work was too advanced and diversified. It sounded to me like a great place to work. Where did you say this place is, Ed?

Hi, my name is Michael Young; sure have a beautiful day, don't we? Can you please tell me where the personnel department is? Yes, I would like to speak to someone about joining the company as a doctoral intern student. I'm in the doctoral program at the University of Detroit; I'm required to undertake a challenging work assignment in industry that will allow me to fulfill the dissertation requirements.

Well, that sure is a generous offer. I'll start as a graduate engineer at full salary just as soon as I finish my undergraduate work? And I'll be allowed to satisfy all of the university requirements while working full time here at Eaton? Sounds great; can't wait to start. By the way, I'm sure you've got plenty of Xerox machines and three-ring binders here, but you don't also happen to have any army personnel carriers, do you?

Got a kid at home and another one on the way and this doctoral stuff is driving me crazy. Dr. Miranda, the way you phrased that last question on the written exam is a bit confusing. The buckling stability of a structural column that theoretically comes to a point like you've shown can't be determined based on the information given. No sir, Dr. Miranda, I still don't think it can be done that way. Then would you allow me to make the following assumptions? No? Then would you allow me to restate my question?

Okay, let me try it this way: What's wrong with you, you moron; any idiot knows that you can't solve that problem the way it's written; why in the hell are you giving me such a hard time anyway?

Yes sir, I'll read your book on the subject.

So the big day is finally here. Elaine found a babysitter so that she can be there for the oral defense of my thesis and I think quite a few other people are going to be there too. As I'm driving toward campus, all my thoughts are on getting this thing done so that I can finally get over this crest and ride the wave as it carries me onto the shore. I know that it will all have been worth it; this is the one big hurdle in my life. From here on it's easy street; no more difficult times ahead for me.

Well, as you can see, the "most optimum" way to control the

servo valve is to dither it with a high-frequency current that will ensure a rapid response time with virtually no stiction. "Most optimum" is a redundant term? Yes sir, Dr. Manos, I stand corrected, but I've always used that term. I guess I've been mistaken.

Yes, that column will buckle when subjected to that input force; I've done a lot of studying on that subject, Dr. Miranda.

Chapter 11
Decisions

Sure do wonder how life would have turned out had I made different decisions at key points along the way. Married someone else? Chosen liberal arts? Joined Ford Motor Company? Better or worse? Good question. I'm glad that I'll never know the answer. Wouldn't want to have regrets, or to think that some of the good things that happened along the way were just the luck of the draw. Maybe life's decisions are like standing in front of the dessert table: many good choices, all different, almost any one would work.

That said, it always seemed like going to work for Eaton Corporation's Engineering and Research Center in Southfield, Michigan, was a good decision. Where else could you find such challenging and diversified projects, state-of-the-art facilities, or better management? Anti-lock brakes, disc brakes for trucks, air bags, materials handling, hydraulics, control systems, transmissions, axles, and solid-state electronics. All of that and much more. And, because our mission was to create advanced new products for the many different divisions of the company, we were always encouraged to think differently and to question the way things were being done. Could we find a better way?

Great job, great company, and the opportunity to work on a major company project that would also satisfy the dissertation requirements for the doctoral program at the University of Detroit. What an opportunity I had been given. Full project engineering status, including pay and benefits, while I pursued the doctoral program at the university. No one I knew had a better arrangement.

It was during those years at Eaton that my creative mind began to explode. As it had been in every other aspect of my life, I found myself in the "question everything" mind-set. Finding a better way to solve technical problems was something that I came to realize I did better than anyone else. I had a deeper insight than others. I could see things in my mind that no one else could see. I always thought in the simplest terms. I was able to assimilate ideas, and I naturally gravitated to practical solutions.

Every one of the projects that passed my way during those years at Eaton was a significant learning experience from both an engineering and a management perspective. Vern, the engineering manager, Lee, the personnel manager, and Bob, the general manager, were all great examples. They did it the way it was supposed to be done, and they taught me a lot.

It was Vern who first promoted me to a supervisory role when I was somewhere around twenty-five years old. I'll never forget the first time I sat down with one of the crusty old senior engineers who suddenly found himself working for me. At somewhere in his fifties, Joe was twice as old as me and probably had five times as many years of experience.

So, Joe, I want you to know that I feel privileged to be working with you. I'm sure that our group can do some great things if we all pull together. I'm asking everyone in the group to always tell me how they feel about things, and I'm committing to always being straightforward with them in return. You may not always agree with me; when you don't, I'm asking that you let me know. I may still see things in a different way, but your thoughts are important to me.

Well, that didn't go too badly; think I'm off to a good start.

Say, Vern, since becoming the chief engineer of this group I've been pretty impressed with everyone except Pete. He just doesn't seem to have the basic engineering or creative skills that we need. I think that his employment should be terminated if things don't change soon. Okay, Vern, that sounds like a reasonable approach. I'll sit down with him at sixty-day intervals and give him a performance review. I'll let him know that if things don't improve we'll have to terminate his employment. Yes, I'll be very clear; there will be no surprises.

Pete, we need to have a conversation about your job performance. I feel that you are making an effort to successfully complete your projects but we're just not seeing the results that we need, so I'd like to sit down with you in about sixty days and review things again. But you need to realize that changes must be made if you are going to remain employed here at Eaton.

Pete, I regret to tell you that I'm still not seeing the improvement that is expected. Let's go through the changes that need to be made so that things will be as clear as possible...and I'd like to sit down with you again in about sixty days. But I need to emphasize that changes are necessary if you are going to remain employed at Eaton.

Pete, this is a difficult conversation to have. For the past four months we've been talking about the need for an improvement in your job performance, but those changes have not been forthcoming. So I regret that we're going to have to make a change in your employment status. We need to go over the separation arrangements that need to be followed...it would be best if you would say your good-byes today and then come back tomorrow to wrap things up. Since tomorrow is Saturday, it will be a little easier to move your things.

Vern, that was one of the most difficult things I've ever done. When I told Pete we were going to terminate his employment, he burst into tears and said that he thought I called him in to give him a raise. He seemed to have no idea that his job was on the line. He told me how hard it was going to be to tell his wife and daughter. And coming in Saturday to supervise his exit was extraordinarily difficult. Just the two of us in the building, and him in tears. Yes, I told him on two previous occasions that his performance had to improve if he was going to remain at Eaton. I thought I had made that very clear.

Maybe I've got a lot more to learn.

The person who had joined you for lunch the week before, whose children were on the Christmas card you received, who waved to you at the grocery store, was the same person you were now rejecting. He was going to be deprived of a paycheck, forced to tell his family and friends that he had failed, and then find a way to pull himself together and start again. Terminating someone's employment would always be the most difficult part of every job that I had, and it never got any easier.

Then there was the time in the mid-1970s when business had fallen off due to a recession. The inevitable decision to significantly reduce employment at the research center left management with the difficult job of identifying the individuals who would need to be terminated and then carrying out the unpleasant task. After lengthy deliberations, and with great secrecy, the poorest-performing individuals were identified and the notification date and time were set.

Eaton's corporate headquarters had approved the termination plan and everything was in order. Supervisors were asked to come to the conference room early that fateful day so that everyone would be ready to talk to those who would be affected at precisely the same time. There we sat; two hours to go, one hour, now thirty minutes. Stomachs were in knots as everyone went over and over in their minds the words they chose to convey the bad news.

It was then, at absolutely the last minute, that Bob, the general manager, walked into the room and announced that corporate headquarters had had a change of mind. He had been told that many of the personnel on the list would have to be changed. Instead of terminating the poorest-performing individuals, the layoff would have to be based strictly on seniority. The possible legal ramifications of laying off employees on any basis other than seniority had spooked the corporate legal staff.

Are you kidding me? We're not dealing with a union here. How can we possibly cut some of our best employees while keeping poorer performers? What an important lesson to learn. Performance doesn't always matter; sometimes it's the luck of the draw. Minutes before you're scheduled to face the firing squad, you get a reprieve and someone else steps into your place. Keep that in mind and always remember how unfair things can be.

But you couldn't blame Bob for that surprising turn of events. He was headed in the right direction but had run into the corporate bureaucracy. Fortunately for those of us at the research center, that didn't happen very often. In most instances corporate allowed our facility to operate independently, which gave Bob a free hand to set up his own policies and procedures, which is exactly what he did.

One of those policies was to allow employees to use virtually all of the company's facilities, after working hours, for their own personal projects. That worked well for me because it meant that I could conveniently work on my own cars in the company's state-of-the-art facility. Car hoists, chain falls, welding equipment, specialized tools, a small parts supply room, and a machine shop were all right there at my fingertips. When you stop and think about it, the company was really putting itself in a risky situation. What if someone had an accident while using the facility?

As you might have guessed, it was only a matter of time before something catastrophic nearly happened to me. It all started when I was about halfway through an ambitious project of replacing the four-cylinder engine in one of my cars with a high-performance eight-cylinder engine from a different vehicle. Countless changes had to be made to fit the new engine and drive train into the vehicle. It seemed like the project was endless; everything that could go wrong did go wrong.

One evening a friend and I were attempting to electric arc weld something to the rear frame area of the vehicle while it was elevated on a hoist in the company's garage. Things weren't going well, however. I was having a problem that welders often encounter: my welding rod was repeatedly sticking to the frame of the vehicle while I was attempting to weld. Pulling back on the rod while wiggling it back and forth would free it, but that process caused a brilliant arc to flash when the rod broke free.

I became more and more frustrated as the rod stuck over and over again. Finally, I angrily pulled back on the sticking rod with such force that when it broke free, my hand flew backward, causing the rod to contact the gas tank, which was right over my head. When the rod hit the gas tank it welded itself again, but this time to the tank. My instantaneous reaction was to pull the rod free once more, but when I did, it created a sizable hole in the tank. Burning gasoline, which had been ignited by the instantaneous electrical flash, began pouring out of the tank, causing the entire work location to go up in flames.

Fortunately, nearby fire extinguishers soon put an end to the potentially disastrous situation. The gas tank hadn't exploded, the

facility was still standing, and we were unhurt. No one other than the two of us was in the building at the time, so the event passed with no one the wiser and our jobs intact.

However, the positive experiences far outweighed the negative.

In the early 1970s I had the good fortune of being Eaton's nominee for the Engineering Society of Detroit's Outstanding Young Engineer of the Year award. This award was given annually to an engineer age thirty-five or younger who was thought to have demonstrated superior engineering and management skills in industry. Candidates representing many highly recognized companies—including General Motors, Ford, Chrysler, Bendix, TRW, Rockwell, and hundreds more—were submitted for consideration.

When I was asked to provide a picture of myself to support the company's nomination, I decided instead to submit a terrific family picture that showed me with my gorgeous wife and two great-looking kids. Seems like that was a good decision, because I heard several positive comments about my family from members of the committee that subsequently interviewed me on different occasions during the selection process.

Being nominated for the award was quite an honor, but the chance of winning against such a strong group of candidates seemed like a long shot at best. But to my surprise, I was selected as one of five finalists. Now my hopes and expectations were up. When the final selection was made, the committee announced that two candidates were equally qualified to be winners, and that they would both receive the award that year. To my delight and surprise, I was one of the two winners. The other winner was an engineering manager from the General Motors Technical Center.

At the engineering society's annual ceremonial dinner, both the GM winner and I were recognized as joint winners of the award, but to my great disappointment it was announced that only one of us could be named the official winner. For some reason the GM guy was selected; I received the joint award but was not recorded as the winner. Bittersweet.

Eaton did many things to create a truly exceptional workplace; too bad I can't mention them all here. But the recollection can't end without mentioning the annual Christmas party that the company sponsored for all employees at an exclusive restaurant on the Detroit River. Dinner, great bands, a fantastic facility, and a very pleasant atmosphere made it an event to really look forward to every year. I remember it as if it happened yesterday. Fantastic music, and dancing with the most beautiful girl in the world.

Where did it go?

I tried to take from the Eaton experience all that I saw that was good. Much of what I had learned eventually ended up at the companies that I would later come to manage. Attitude, communication methods, management techniques, and a sense of employee appreciation. All, I hope, can still be found on the path that led from Eaton.

Chapter 12
Don't Want You Here

With the doctoral program behind me, several Eaton promotions under my belt, and the Engineering Society of Detroit award sitting on a shelf in my office, I suddenly found myself in a very comfortable place. I was working for a company that I loved and my bills were getting paid. Would have been a great time to take a breather, but that was something I had never known how to do.

So when I received a phone call one day from the vice president of personnel of Rockwell International's Automotive Operations I was interested in what he had to say. He asked if I would talk to Rockwell about the director of product development position that they had open. Said he was calling on behalf of William P, president of Automotive Operations. He reminded me that William P had also won the Engineering Society of Detroit's Outstanding Young Engineer of the Year award, which gave the two of us something in common.

What harm could there be in talking?

When I showed up for my first job interview, I was impressed with how much everyone seemed to like me. The president of the operation, the vice president of engineering, and countless other key figures in the organization had bent over backwards to sell me on the opportunity. The only person I didn't feel I connected with was a guy named Stan, the person to whom I would report if I joined their organization. That certainly was a concern, but that concern seemed to get buried beneath the positive responses that I had gotten from all of the others.

I returned several times for additional interviews, and the feedback that I received continued to be positive. The only trouble that I was running into was that Stan was out of town during each of my subsequent visits. Not to worry, I was told; Stan really wants you to come.

When Rockwell extended a formal offer of employment, it seemed clear that everyone in the organization, including Stan, must have felt comfortable with me. Okay, so I guess I misunderstood Stan's feelings. I was sure we could find a way to work together successfully.

Rockwell had the reputation of paying its employees well. That was important, because there was no reason for me to leave Eaton if I wasn't going to make a lot more money. The first offer that Rockwell made was good but not good enough, so I turned it down. Several improved offers followed, but I turned all of them down as well. It seemed clear at one point that the Rockwell job just wasn't going to happen. It was then that Elaine and I decided to go ahead with the plans that we had put on hold to build a new home in Brighton, Michigan, an hour's drive from Rockwell, which was too far.

Wasn't long after we committed to the new home that Rockwell unexpectedly improved their offer to the level that I had previously insisted on. But the new home was just too far from Rockwell, so I turned it down again. However, Rockwell just wouldn't take no for an answer. Next thing I knew I had an even better offer; I took the job.

When I showed up for my first day at work, I immediately got the feeling that something wasn't right. From the very start, the place seemed cold and disconnected. That might have been because everything was new and different, but something told me that it was more than that. Stan, my new boss, was out of town the morning that I showed up for work, so I was pretty much on my own from the start. He was due in later that day. The first thing I did that morning was to call a meeting of the management group that reported to me so we could begin the process of getting to know each other. The meeting went reasonably well, but I still had the feeling that something just wasn't right.

Immediately after that first meeting, two of my direct reports asked if they could talk to me in private. Sure, I said, what's on your mind? Mike, they said, we're not sure how to tell you this, but we feel you need to know what's going on. Go ahead, I said, what's the problem? Stan told us all that you were hired against his wishes. When he was out of town, Bob G, the vice president of engineering, scheduled your additional job interviews. Stan was against hiring you from the start. Your employment offer went out without his approval while he was traveling.

Oh my god, what did I get myself into? I've got a family to feed and a new house to pay for. What am I going to do now?

Later that day, Stan finally did show up. His office was right next to mine, so I saw him as soon as he walked in. Surely he would try to make the best of a bad situation, wouldn't he? What could he do other than try to make this thing work out one way or another?

He hardly had time to take off his coat before he asked if I would come into his office. Not a handshake; not hello, how are you; not good to see you; not welcome to Rockwell. Just come into my office; go ahead, close the door.

Not the kind of start I was hoping for, but it immediately got much worse. I had not even gotten seated when Stan shot his arm out and pointed his finger right in my face. I didn't want you here, he yelled. Bob G hired you without my approval. He may be my boss, but you work for me. I don't want you here.

Hi, Elaine, I'm calling with some really bad news. My boss, Stan, just told me that…

That first chaotic day led to a terrible night of soul searching.

What was I going to do now? How long can we make ends meet if I'm out of a job? Should I try to go back to Eaton?

The next day when I came in to work, I had a note on my desk to see Bob G, the vice president of engineering, ASAP. Bob had been traveling on my first day at work, so this was his first opportunity to talk to me. What was I going to say to him? What the hell's going on, Bob? You hired me to work for a guy who doesn't want me? Fuck you?

None of that was necessary. As I walked into his office, Bob extended his hand to greet me and was as pleasant as he could be. He immediately apologized for what he already knew Stan had said to me. Not to worry, he said. He was going to fire Stan and I was going to take his place. That's why he had hired me against Stan's wishes. If I would be patient for a little while, everything would work out fine.

Hi, Elaine, I'm calling with some really good news. Bob G, the vice president of engineering, just told me that…

I had dodged a bullet that was headed straight for me, or so I thought. A couple of days later, the vice president of personnel showed up in my office with some very bad news. Bob had just suffered a massive heart attack and was in the hospital. According to the hospital, he was not going to live much longer.

You're kidding me, right? Tell me this is all a joke. Tell me!

Hi, Elaine, I'm calling with some really bad news. The vice president of personnel just told me that…

The next day I was sitting in my office in utter despair when the personnel director showed up. Bob was near death, he said, but he had asked the vice president of personnel to come to the hospital with a tape recorder. Before Bob died, he was going to tape-record a directive to fire Stan. The vice president was on his way to the hospital at that very moment. Hopefully he would get there in time.

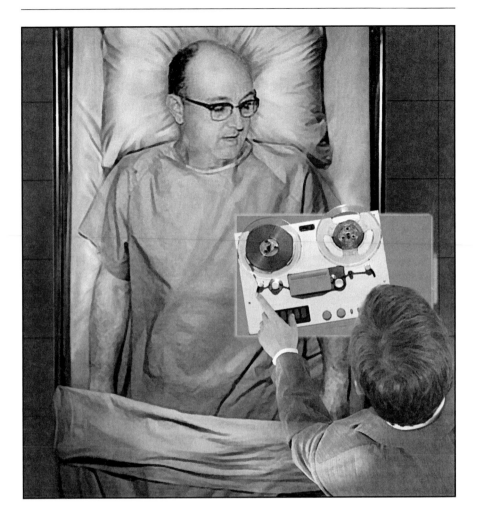

He did. The recording was made. Bob died. Stan got fired. I survived.

Hi, Elaine, I'm calling with some really bad and some really good news. Bob G just...

Several years later I was talking to the personnel director who had once given me the news about the tape-recorded firing of Stan.

We had become good friends by that time and he was comfortable telling me more about the circumstances of my hiring and Stan's subsequent firing. One thing that I never understood was why Rockwell had tried so hard to hire me even though I repeatedly had turned them down. Five minutes later my friend was showing me my personnel file and a copy of the résumé that I had submitted when I had been interviewed. On my résumé in large red print was a note from William P, the president, that said: *Hire him!!!!!! William P!!!!!!*

When the big boss spoke, the organization followed orders. As the story goes, William P insisted that the organization find a way to get me, whatever it took. I didn't know it at the time, but I probably could have asked for almost anything and I would have gotten it.

But the Rockwell tale is just getting started. Stan and Bob were both gone, but William P, the president and my Outstanding Young Engineer of the Year colleague, was still there. Still there, but not for long. The next thing I knew, he left Rockwell to take over as president of Bendix Corporation. I found little consolation in the fact that he later asked me to interview for a job at Bendix. No thanks, Bill; I don't think I can go through another period of absolute insanity.

At the time I was thirty-three years old and was probably just too young to be seriously considered for the vice president of engineering job that Bob had left behind. In any case, Skip W, the new president of Rockwell Automotive, hired a guy from outside the organization to be the new engineering vice president and my boss. Joe M was an American who had previously worked in France for Chrysler Corporation. Chrysler Corporation? Seemed to be a bad omen right from the start.

Bad attitude on my part, that's for sure. But, as was usually the case, my instincts were right. Joe turned out to be the worst person I ever worked for. He was extremely paranoid; he saw a conspiracy in everything that happened around him and acted like everyone was out to get him. The funny thing was that his last name, which will go unmentioned, translates to "evil" in Latin.

Because I did my job so well, Joe didn't have the strength to get rid of me. I think he wanted that more than anything, but he just couldn't pull it off. I needed to be constantly on my guard to never break the rules or give him any cause to bring action against me. What did I do to deserve this?

Several years later something happened that led to a showdown between the two of us. It so happened that before joining Rockwell I had started working on a truly revolutionary new electromechanical device for accurately measuring the fuel consumption rate of an automobile. The Autocomputer was a device that gave drivers instantaneous miles per gallon readings while they were driving, as well as information on vehicle speed, distance traveled, and gallons of fuel consumed. There was nothing else like it at the time.

I had spent a great deal of my personal time and money on the project, and at the time I joined Rockwell I had the Autocomputer far enough along that I was demonstrating it to automotive companies and their suppliers. In addition, I had strong patent coverage on the device. At the time of my employment, I had obtained a written agreement that I was free to continue working on the project outside of Rockwell.

One of the Rockwell division vice presidents had gotten interested in the Autocomputer and wanted to obtain the rights to the product for Rockwell. That would have been a great outcome for me, because it could have led to commercialization of the device and substantial financial benefit to me.

Everything appeared to be in order as we began drafting a legal agreement between the parties. It was then that things suddenly veered off track. Unexpectedly, I was called into Joe's office one morning to discuss ownership rights to the Autocomputer. Sitting with Joe in his office was a corporate attorney whom I had never met before. On Joe's desk sat a legal document that said I was relinquishing all rights to the Autocomputer since I had worked on the product while I was a Rockwell employee. In their opinion, I had forfeited my rights to the company, and I was not entitled to any compensation.

I explained over and over again that the project had begun well before I joined Rockwell, that I had a written agreement that said I could continue working on the project, and that Rockwell had absolutely no rights unless I was satisfactorily compensated. It was all to no avail. I was threatened with employment termination because I would not sign the agreement.

Then go ahead and terminate my employment, because I'm not going to sign it. You guys can both go fuck yourselves! I'm going back to my office; just let me know what you decide you want to do.

That's exactly how it happened, and that's exactly what I said. I did go back to my office, but nothing was ever said again about the issue. I never saw the attorney again. Joe never brought up the subject again. I remained an employee, and Rockwell never went further with the project.

It wasn't long after the Autocomputer incident that Joe stuck his head in my office to ask if I would accompany him on a walk through the machine shop. He said he had just gotten an anonymous phone call from someone who told him that "government work" was going on in the machine shop and that the two of us needed to check that out.

"Government work" is the term used to describe personal work that is being done on the company's premises, usually in secret. The machine shop's main function is to produce the prototype parts for projects that are being developed by the company. If someone were using the company's facilities to work on a personal project, it could lead to termination of employment, maybe even the guillotine.

Joe was on the case. He was almost jubilant at the thought of catching someone red-handed. Although he didn't say it, it was evident to me that he thought I might be the person who had commissioned the "government work." Wouldn't that have been interesting?

What would we find out there; someone working on a car engine? Seemed like all of the car nuts working at Rockwell at one time or another had done some level of work on their own projects. Sometimes it was just about the only place you could get it done. I knew that, and I knew that Joe knew that.

And I knew that Joe had run many "government jobs" at different times and places. But the chance to catch someone in the act, especially if that someone was me, would have been almost too good to be true.

As we quickly walked out to the machine shop, Joe was licking his chops. When we entered, we didn't tell anyone why we were there. Let's just look at all the work benches, pick-up tables, and machines. Any sign of an exhaust manifold, carburetor, piston, or anything else that obviously came off someone's car? Nothing over here, nothing over there. Don't see anything on that machine, or that one either. Damn! Joe didn't see anything at all. What a letdown. He thought he was going to hit on something big, so he was really disappointed.

He had found nothing. Absolutely nothing.

About sixty seconds after we had returned to our offices, I spun on my heels and raced back out to the machine shop at full speed. Getting all that shit out of there was mission imperative. It was over there, and over there, and over there too. It was on that machine and that one too. Get that goddamn stuff out of here now! Right now!

Joe had missed it. He missed it because he didn't know what he was looking for. All he could think of was auto parts. He was looking for auto parts because that's what he used to run through the shop himself. He was probably the master of government work but his work had been automotive-related. He couldn't recognize Autocomputer parts even when he was looking right at them, up close and personal. Not one or two, but countless numbers. He just didn't know what he was looking at. He missed the call.

He had me by the balls but didn't know it. All he had to do was squeeze!

My oh my, it just doesn't get any more breathtaking than that, does it? But of course there's always one more story to tell.

It all started one day when I was sitting in my office and my assistant buzzed to tell me that someone who worked for me was outside my office asking to speak to me. Since I always had an open-door policy, I invited her in. She sat down in a chair across from my desk and began telling me about a work problem. After about five minutes she stopped in the middle of her sentence and said nothing for about thirty seconds. Then she said, "I want to fuck you!"

Say whaaaat?!

I could see this was going to be trouble. "You've got to understand that that kind of conversation is inappropriate. Is there anything more concerning the problem you came to see me about?"

The conversation ended with an apology. However, several days later I found written on different pages of my daily calendar the words "I want to fuck you." I sure as hell didn't write it, but it wasn't hard to guess who did. But how could anyone have gotten into my office, anyway?

A few days later my assistant buzzed me again to say that the same person was back wanting to talk to me again. Damn, I never told my assistant about the incident because that would have been awkward. Too late now; ask her to come in. The conversation started with another apology about what had been said on the previous occasion, but it wasn't long before there was another unexpected pause. "I want to fuck you," she said.

Not sure what I said then, but it wasn't long before I had her out of my office and I was on my way to the personnel department. What do I do now, fellas?

After a few more days had passed I was beginning to think that the issue was behind me, but that wasn't the case. An agitated personnel director popped into my office one morning to tell me that the "I want to fuck you girl" had shown up that day with a revolver and was threatening other employees. By that time the police had come and she had been escorted off to jail without further incident.

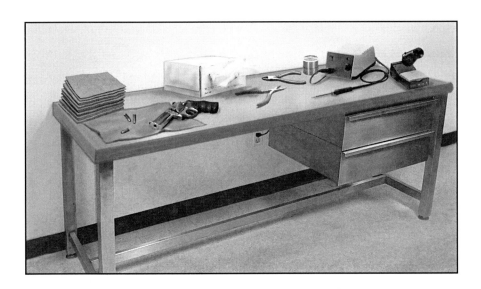

Say whaaaat?!

A week or two later we all heard that the gunslinger had subsequently been locked up in a mental institution and that she would never be back at work. What a relief! Now let's get on with the other business at hand.

The office that I used at that time was built in an interior portion of the building so I had no windows and no natural light coming into the office. Unfortunately, the construction crew that originally remodeled my office had never modified the electrical system to relocate a light switch near the entrance door. Therefore, every morning it was necessary for me to grope my way in the dark from the entrance door to the light switch, which was located on the far side of the office.

I usually started work early in those days, often an hour or more before most others had arrived. One morning I came in early to get a fast start on the day. I opened the door and with my hand outstretched began trying to find my way across the room. I couldn't see a thing, but when I finally got to where I expected the light switch to be, I heard a quiet, shaky voice in front of me call out, "Why did you do that?"

Say whaaaat?!

It was pitch black and I couldn't see anything or anyone in the room. What in the hell was going on? When I finally got the light on I could see the "I want to fuck you girl," the gunslinger,

sitting in a fetal position with her arms wrapped tightly around her legs, rocking forward and back while moaning, "Why did you do that?" Her face was red and extremely agitated. It didn't look good. "Why did you do that?"

"Why did I do what?" I asked.

Why had I told all those people that she was selling drugs? Why had I put a tape recorder under the seat in her car? Why had I gone on Walter Cronkite's CBS national news to tell everyone in the country about her? Question after question, while she rocked back and forth with her hands wrapped around her legs.

This was the same person who had brought a gun in to work, wasn't it? Seemed reasonable to worry that she had a gun with her then, too.

Think fast, how had Hopalong Cassidy wrestled the gun away from those bad guys that one time? Watch closely for her to make any sudden movement. Be prepared to launch yourself toward her while keeping clear of the gun she might be carrying. You were relatively young at the time, so you could probably have pulled it off. Just like Hopalong.

Wish I could say that I did something heroic, but nothing like that turned out to be necessary. There was no gun. After about half an hour I calmly picked up the phone to call personnel. She was later escorted away without further incident and returned to the mental facility where she had been held. Whatever I had said to her seemed to calm things down.

So why don't you ask me if anything interesting ever happened while I worked at Rockwell?

Just gotta wrap this up on a positive note. Years after leaving Rockwell, I had gotten myself into the position of CEO of York International, the largest independent heating, ventilating, air-conditioning, and refrigeration company in the world. As CEO I had operations throughout the world reporting to me. As it turns out, there came a time when I needed to find someone to take over as president of our French operations. Our human resources department was on the job and the search was under way.

Then it occurred to me that my old nemesis Joe M had repeat-edly told me, and everyone else, for that matter, that he had loved the time he had spent living in France while he was working for Chrysler. So much so that he always wished he could return to work in France someday. The chance to settle the score with Joe had presented itself at last.

Sounds petty, doesn't it? After all those years to still hold a grudge. To contemplate actually going way out of my way to even things up is childish, isn't it? Certainly someone who was then run-ning one of the largest corporations in the country would never do such a thing, would he?

Bring him in for several interviews. Make him want the job so bad. Then have the pleasure of telling him no.

Would the CEO of a Fortune 500 company do that?

You bet!

Chapter 13

You All Come Down and See Us, Now

If you've never seen the Appalachian Mountains in northeast Tennessee and southwest Virginia, you've really missed something. Mountains not so high that the trees won't grow, nor so far north that all you see is evergreens. Not a place where they speak a different language, although *you all* need to pay attention to the regional nature of the language and the accent. An area of the country where people work hard and open their hearts to the strangers who can accept who they are, but can slam the door shut if you start acting like one of them damn Yankees: "You're not from around here, are you?"

Family is just about the number one most important thing around here. That, and the church, you know. In fact, most of my relatives live just "over yonder," past that valley over there. Most of us never did much traveling, but Aunt Sara once took a trip

across the country to see what all that California talk was about. Come to think of it, Uncle Ray once took a trip to Ireland to see where our relatives came from. I ain't never been much farther than Missouri myself, though; just can't seem to take time away from my job or our farm. So you say you're going to be working at that Bristol Compressors plant just north of town, eh? Two of my cousins work there. They say business is awfully slow lately; rumor is that they might have another layoff. What did you say your job over there was again?

Vice president of engineering and quality control. We just moved here from Rockwell Automotive Operations in Michigan. Yes, the same Rockwell that built the space shuttle, but that was the Aerospace Division. We bought a home near Goosepimple Junction, over by the country club. Where in the world did that name come from, anyway?

After about two weeks on the new job I was going to get a chance to meet the Bristol board of directors at a Friday-night dinner following one of their meetings. This was going to be a chance to size everyone up and try to make a good first impression. Wear the right suit, shirt, and tie, everything neatly pressed, shiny shoes, clean shave, and looking sharp. I was ready, and everything went well. First impressions only happen once.

That dinner meeting had lasted well into the night, so I was glad that I had the weekend to prepare for a high-level Monday-morning meeting with our largest and most important supplier, A. O. Smith, in Cincinnati. I would be ready for my early-morning connecting flight. This would be another chance to try to make a good first impression.

As it happened, I must have set my alarm clock improperly, because I overslept that Monday morning. When I finally opened my eyes and looked at the alarm, I realized that there was almost no time before my flight was scheduled to leave. Getting to the airport in time to catch that plane appeared to be an impossibility, but I decided to try anyway.

Out of bed with no time even to take a piss. Threw on my suit pants, threw on my shirt but didn't button it. Grabbed my belt, tie, socks, and suit jacket but didn't take the time to put on any of them. Shoes untied, toiletries in hand, I was in the car and on my hundred-mile-per-hour race to the airport. I would have to clean myself up and get organized during my layover in Charlotte.

I raced from my car to the counter and from the counter to the gate. I couldn't believe it. I got there just as they were about to close the door. There I was, stumbling down the aisle of the plane, looking for my seat, wondering what the other passengers thought about the bum who had just gotten onto their plane.

Shirt unbuttoned and out of my pants, shoes untied with no socks, unshaven, hair not combed, teeth not brushed, belt, tie, and socks in hand, I saw the vacant seat that had my number on it. And then I realized that in the seat next to mine sat one of our prominent directors, George B.

Oh…hi…George…I guess I should explain…

Don't worry, Rod, I'm sure I'll be able to get along with Art okay. I'll bring him into our engineering meetings whenever that is appropriate. His opinion matters to me, so I don't think we'll have any problem working together. I understand what you're saying and I can appreciate how he must feel, having founded the company, overseen the design of its products, and then been shuffled off to the side when you took over. I do understand that type of personality and there's no way I'll let him interfere with my operations. Trust me, everything will work out fine.

Maybe sometime in the distant future, Rod, I'll tell you about the interview that I had with Art when I first visited Bristol. That chain-smoking tough old Dutchman was relentlessly quizzing me on engineering matters when he suddenly broke into an extreme coughing fit that would not stop. It was so severe that Art couldn't catch his breath and his face was turning purple. I've never seen anything like it. It went on for at least five minutes and I didn't know what to do. The man looked like he was dying right there in front of me. He simply couldn't catch his breath. Talk about awkward. Do I stare at him or look up at the ceiling? Do I jump across the desk to administer mouth-to-mouth resuscitation or do I call an ambulance?

With that as a starting point, I'm pretty sure I can handle anything else that comes my way as it pertains to Art.

As the overseer of all engineering and quality control operations at Bristol Compressors, I had been able to get a good sense
of the production operations during the first year on the job. And
the better I understood the operations, the more I could see the
potential for the future. There was as much capital equipment
at Bristol as at any of our competitors, but everything was vastly
underutilized. We had the capability to produce far more product
without significantly increasing our capital expenditures. That was
a good thing because our financial condition was weak. In fact, if
business took a little bit of a dip, we could have been in serious
financial trouble.

Rod's efforts to open up markets for Bristol in the Middle East
and elsewhere, and the product cost reductions that we had started
to implement, were leading to increasing orders and greater manufacturing volume. The problem was that Dan, our operations VP,
didn't have a clue as to how to quickly and efficiently increase production capacity in the plant. He seemed to think that we were
already near full capacity. He just didn't get it.

On repeated occasions I told Rod that I believed we could
quickly grow our manufacturing capacity to keep up with our
growing sales if we implemented a number of significant changes
in our operations.

Thanks for the confidence that you and the board of directors have shown in me, Rod. At age thirty-nine I feel privileged to have the chance to succeed you as president of Bristol Compressors and to become a member of the board of directors. I'm confident that I can lead this company to the highest level of success.

If you have any difficulty hearing me in the back of the room, please raise your hand. First, I would like to thank Rod and the board of directors for giving me the opportunity to lead this fine

company. Second, I would like to thank every one of you for the job that you do here at Bristol Compressors. I feel privileged to work with all of you.

I want you all to know that I believe we are at the beginning of a period of tremendous growth and prosperity, the likes of which will be truly impressive. My vision of the future starts with you, our company's most valuable asset. What you and I do as employees of Bristol will separate us from our competition and will allow us to become the leader in our industry. The difference between our company and our competition is our workforce and our management methods. They have the same bricks and mortar that we have. They have the same kinds of machines that we have. They have everything that we have except our workforce, our attitude, and our management excellence. Those are our great advantages. If you are willing to give this company your very best, and if our company adopts management principles that put you first, then we cannot help but succeed.

To capitalize on our strengths, I want to create an organization that has outstanding communications throughout. Not just communications from me to you but also from you to me. Not just communications within groups but also between groups. Everyone needs to hear and to be heard. Everyone needs to understand as much about the company's operations as possible. And supervision must hear what you think we need to do to make this the best-running company possible.

Facilitating good communications is not easy. It requires a

major commitment of time and energy by all supervisory personnel. And it requires patience and understanding on your part: not
everything that you want or suggest will be doable, and many things
will not be achievable in short order. But as imperfect as the process
is, our company will benefit immensely as a result of our efforts.

To that end, I will meet with all employees on a quarterly basis
to keep everyone updated on our company's operations and our
performance. In those meetings I'll tell you everything that I possibly can about our progress, our problems, and our profitability. I
will always be honest with you and I ask the same thing in return.

And I will listen. Tell me what you think. What can we do to
make your job, your department, and our company operate more
smoothly? On a regular basis I will also meet with a randomly
selected group of employees in a conference room to exchange ideas.
I'll be out on the shop floor visiting every department, on every
shift, in an effort to make myself as accessible as possible. When I
see you, you can be sure that I will acknowledge your presence with
a sincere smile, a hello, and an expression of appreciation for the
contribution you are making to our company. I expect that all levels
of supervision will implement similar communications practices.

Notice to All Employees: I am pleased to tell you that in the
coming year, and in the years to follow, our company will regularly
schedule four social events to which all employees and their families will be invited.

- Just prior to our Christmas break, we will hold a children's Christmas party. At this party, every child eighteen years and younger will be given a beautifully wrapped and personalized gift that you will have chosen from a gift catalog provided prior to the party. There will be games, special activities, workshops, props, decorations, and music. And Santa Claus will be there to say hi to everyone.
- In that same time frame, we will also schedule an adult Christmas party for all employees. This party will be a first-class event that will include dinner, music, and entertainment. You won't want to miss it.
- During the early summer months, we will have a company picnic at which we will have adult and children's games and sporting events, swimming, and a first-class meal.
- In the early fall, we will have a family open house here at our facility. Bring your partner and your children to our plant so that you can show them where you work and what we do here at Bristol Compressors. A buffet lunch and soft drinks will be provided.

We'll be looking for volunteers to help set up all of these events; your willingness to participate would be greatly appreciated.

When I took over as president three months ago I told you that I would meet on a quarterly basis with all employees of the company. This is the second of those meetings; others will follow without fail. Our goal is to keep you fully informed about our company's initiatives and the progress that we are making in attaining our goals. The first thing I would like to talk about today is our company's number-one operational priority: new product development.

The products that we are producing today are competitive in the marketplace. Our efficiencies, reliability, sound levels, and costs are all near those of our competition. That's both a good and a bad thing. It's good because we do have a product that our customers want to buy. It's bad, however, because we don't offer much that is better than our competition. Our customers can just as easily buy from our competitors as they can from us. In fact, because our competitors are far better established in the marketplace, they often will be the customer's first choice as a supplier, if all else is equal. If we are going to change that, we are going to have to offer them products that are notably better than our competition's. That's why we need to focus a great deal of our attention and our resources on new product development. Nothing, absolutely nothing, is more important to our company's long-term prosperity than the development of products that are vastly superior to what our competition has to offer.

As many of you know by now, my educational background is in engineering. I have spent a great deal of my professional life in new product development and I have been a part of many highly successful advancements in the field of product design. I want you to know that our engineering department has been working hard from the very first day I joined the company as vice president of engineering and quality control just over one year ago to take a major step forward in our product line's performance. The first round of product improvements that we will soon introduce will allow us to leapfrog our competition in three important areas: efficiency, reliability, and cost. You will all soon see major product line changes being implemented in the production areas of our company as our new 23 series product is introduced. Much more is to follow in very short order. In fact, an entirely new product, which will be called the Inertia compressor, will be introduced in about one year. This new product is so advanced that it will revolutionize the industry. Hang on to your hat; the ride is just beginning.

When we first began these quarterly communications meetings about a year ago I told you that we had a great future and that I had every expectation that our business would grow rapidly. You can now see that growth all around you; many new full-time employees have joined our company as a result of this growth. The new products that we recently introduced and the operational changes that we have made throughout the company are some of the reasons our sales volume has expanded so rapidly. From a financial standpoint we have made a major turnaround. We are now profitable enough that we have been able to pay down a significant portion of our debt load, which puts us in a much stronger position than we were in, in the past. You are the reason why we are prospering. The pay raises that were recently implemented companywide are just one of the ways the company has of recognizing the contribution that you have made, and of thanking you for your effort. But the best is still ahead of us; we've only just begun.

I would like to begin today's board meeting with some positive news. We are now close enough to the end of our year that we are able to forecast record profits for this year, and based on our projected orders for next year, to forecast a further dramatic improvement in next year's profitability. We'll get into those details as the meeting progresses.

What I want to talk about now, however, is a proposal that I would like to make to the board to immediately implement a major new profit-sharing plan for all employees, to be paid just before the Christmas break in about three weeks. My proposal is to give all employees a bonus check in the amount of several thousand dollars. Every employee would receive the same level of compensation with no exceptions; I and my senior staff would be excluded. For hourly production employees this bonus could amount to as much as 20 percent of their base wages. I realize this is an unusual request to make and I also realize that it will be a considerable cost to the company. What I have not yet told you is that the record profit level that I have forecast for this year already reflects the cost of this action. If the board decides against this proposal, our profit level for this year will be greater than what I previously forecast.

When I took over the leadership of this company I told our workforce that we had a bright future and that if they would give this company their best effort they would share in the better times that would be ahead of us. Rest assured that I have never suggested to anyone that there would ever be a supplemental bonus program, so they have absolutely no knowledge of what I am now proposing; only several members of my direct staff have been involved in this discussion. But I believe the time has now come to share this company's prosperity with our workforce. This is not something that we *must* do, but it is the thing that we *should* do.

Confidential memo to the Bristol Compressors Board of Directors: I am pleased to tell you that the supplemental bonus checks that we distributed to all employees the last work day before Christmas break were extremely well received. It is difficult to put into words the positive reaction that was expressed in many different ways across the entire workforce. It is a fact that many employees broke down with tears in their eyes when they realized what had just happened. Many said that the bonus would allow them to buy Christmas presents for their kids or to keep their utilities on a while longer. From all the employees at Bristol Compressors, I would like to express the deepest appreciation to the board for their very generous support.

Business was booming, due in part to the fact that we were opening new markets for our products all around the world. Once Chuck H, our VP of sales and marketing, and I were traveling on one of Japan's bullet trains, to call on several potential new customers. At some point along the way we decided to stop in the dining car to get something to eat and drink.

The dining car was compact. Narrow tables with cramped bench seats were wedged into the confined space. It was common practice to share these tables with complete strangers so that as many people could be accommodated as possible.

With our food and drinks in hand, Chuck and I approached a table at which a distinguished older Japanese couple were sitting. We looked at the couple and gestured in some way to ask if we could be seated. A reserved nod led to our setting our items down on the narrow table and then squeezing ourselves into the space directly opposite the couple. They didn't smile or show any other signs of friendliness. Oh well, I thought, let's just eat and get out of here as fast as we can.

We had hardly gotten seated before disaster struck. While Chuck was reaching for something on the table, he inadvertently knocked his glass of water off the table and onto the lap of the lady sitting across from us. Oh, no, anything but that! How embarrassing! Everyone at the table scrambled to clean up the mess. As Chuck and I apologized over and over again, we received hostile glares from the couple, who had to be thinking, "How in the hell did we ever lose a war to these people?"

All I could think about was the extremely embarrassing situation that we had just created. Get me out of here, please. But not so fast. As Chuck was mopping up the last of the water on the table he knocked a large glass of Coke off the table and right onto the lap of the same lady.

I'm not kidding.

As we went into full cleanup mode for the second time, I was wondering how, in the Japanese language, you could say, "I don't know this guy; he just happened to be wandering down the aisle behind me."

Thank you all for being here for another of our quarterly communications meetings. I've got some important news to share with all of you. Because our sales volume has continued to grow so rapidly, we now find ourselves at full, three-shift, Monday through Friday plant capacity. We've implemented many changes during the past three years in all areas of manufacturing, engineering, purchasing, and materials handling to increase our productive capacity. The fact is that we are now producing more than ten times as many compressors per year as we did three years ago. And we've done it without dramatically increasing the size of our facility.

To keep up with increasing demand, however, we must now either invest heavily in a facility expansion or find another way to even more fully utilize our existing facility. The only way I know to do that is to work our facility twenty-four hours per day, seven days per week. In other words, to never shut this plant down, except for holidays. I don't know how best to implement twenty-four-hour, seven-day operations, so I am asking all of you to think about how that can be done in a way that would work best for our workforce and be as cost effective as possible.

Confidential memo to the Bristol Compressors Board of Directors: As you heard at several of our most recent board meetings, we have been working to develop a plan that would allow us to utilize our facility on a twenty-four-hour-per-day, seven-day-per-week basis. I am now able to update you on our plans to implement this new work schedule. For your information, this work schedule was originally proposed by one of our hourly employees during a regularly scheduled quarterly communications meeting. In short, we will have regularly scheduled, back to back, twelve-hour work shifts. All shifts will work eighty-four hours in every two-week period; on average forty-two hours per week. Two of those forty-two hours will be at time and one half overtime pay, which is required by law. The details of this new work schedule are as follows…

Well, Rod, this was always the plan, wasn't it? To get this company in good enough shape to sell out to a strong buyer who could help it attain an even more prosperous future. And now York International is waving a fistful of money in our face because they want Bristol Compressors to be part of their air-conditioning, heating, refrigeration, and air-handling business. It will be a bit difficult emotionally to say good-bye to our current board; all of you have been really great to work with. I hope that York International will be able to provide the boost that this company will need to allow it to reach the next level.

Can you hear me in the back of the room? Okay; good. I am pleased to inform you that York International, the world's largest independent air-conditioning, heating, refrigeration, and air-handling company, has just purchased Bristol Compressors. I am also pleased to tell you that York has asked me to stay on as president and CEO of Bristol Compressors. We will become one of the independent operating divisions within the York organization. This is a very positive step for our company, one that will allow us to continue our strong growth pattern in the future.

When we were purchased by York International approximately one year ago, I told you at one of our quarterly communications meetings that we expected to continue our strong growth pattern as part of an independent division of the York organization. We have done that to an extent that has amazed everyone in the York organization. It would be an understatement to say that they are pleased with their purchase of our company. We are now one of the most profitable divisions in the York organization. Thank you all for your hard work and the contribution you have made to the success that we are enjoying as a company.

I am also pleased to tell you that York International has asked me to assume the position of president and chief operating officer and to become a member of the board of directors of the parent company. I will relocate to York, Pennsylvania; Bristol Compressors will continue to report to me in this new capacity, as will all of the other York International operations. Joe L, our current vice president of engineering and quality assurance, will succeed me as president and chief executive officer of Bristol Compressors.

Know that Bristol Compressors will always hold the nearest and dearest place in my heart. Thank you all for the support and friendship that you have extended to me during these past few years. Our next goal is to become the most profitable business in the entire HVAC industry, as measured as a percentage of sales. I am confident that Joe L can lead us there in the next few years.

Chapter 14

Let's Make
a Deal

During the 1980s the buying and selling of major corporations reached full stride in the business world: corporate buyouts and mergers were taking place in industry at an alarming rate. Many of these new acquisitions were made on a highly leveraged basis, which simply means that the purchasing entity borrowed a large portion of the transaction price while simultaneously investing only a small portion of its own equity capital. Lenders seemed to gravitate to these highly leveraged transactions, often because the dealmakers themselves stood to personally profit. But most often the biggest winners were the financial visionaries who put these deals together; if they could buy a company with little of their own equity capital invested, they stood to profit handsomely if the company could subsequently be sold again in the future at a reasonable profit. The more highly leveraged the deal, the higher the return *rate* they would realize if they were successful. If they were unsuccessful and the acquired company failed, they lost relatively little because they had not put much of their own capital into the deal. The biggest losers were often the acquired company's employees: they might become the innocent victims of a careless transaction that had gone bad. Welcome to the rough-and-tumble world of the leveraged buyout, or LBO.

Bristol Compressors, York International, and Evcon Industries, all companies that I headed up, were LBO companies at one time or another. The two different investor groups who originally purchased both Bristol and Evcon did so on a highly leveraged basis, which resulted in relatively high debt loads that each company had to service. Fortunately, both businesses subsequently prospered, and when they were sold again the initial investors realized a substantial profit on their deals. Coincidentally, it was York International that bought both companies from the original LBO investors in unrelated transactions at different times: Bristol in 1987 and Evcon in 1995. In the time between these two purchases, York International itself was sold in an LBO transaction in 1989.

I was president, CEO, and chairman of the board at the time Bristol Compressors was sold to York International. By the time of that sale, Bristol had become a powerful competitor in the HVAC industry. Fortunately, the York board asked me to continue heading up the company under their new ownership. And one year after the Bristol acquisition, the York board asked if I would take over leadership of York itself, the parent company. However, at the time I was offered the job of president, chief operating officer, and board member, I was informed that the board intended to put York up for sale and that it was possible that new owners would want someone of their own choosing to head up the corporation. Did I

want to take this new job under those tenuous circumstances? The answer was yes.

Timing can sometimes be everything, it seems. Just before making a public announcement of York's change in leadership and the board's intention to put the company up for sale, word inadvertently leaked out that those changes were imminent. Immediately the news flashed through the investment community, and the price of York stock on the New York Stock Exchange skyrocketed. When a major corporation like York is put up for sale, or when key management changes are made, the price of the company's stock frequently goes up in anticipation of increased stockholder interest. That is the main reason why information concerning major changes is not to be shared with the investment community until the day of the official announcement.

The jump in share price had negative consequences for me because part of my new compensation package included a substantial stock option grant whose exercise price was determined by the price of the company's stock on the day I officially took over my new position. Since the share price shot up the day before the announcement, the exercise price of my new options was much higher than it would have been one day earlier. As it turned out, the chairman of the York board was the person who had inadvertently let the investment community know about the changes prior to the public announcement. I was subsequently assured by the chairman that the company would "make it up to me" in some way in the future. Unfortunately, things were moving too fast; nothing was ever done to correct the situation. But, since the share price continued to climb, my options were still attractive.

Selling a business is a lot like selling a home. Usually an agent or Realtor represents the seller. When a business is sold, an investment banker frequently represents the company that is putting itself up for sale. It is the banker's job to find prospective buyers and then manage the sale process. Often one of their primary responsibilities is to assist the buyer in structuring complex, multilevel financing arrangements, which necessitates the participation of an endless number of financial organizations and legal firms. But, of course, that's all required if a few privileged people are going to get very rich.

When the York board decided to put the company up for sale, it partnered with Merrill Lynch, one of the leading investment banking firms at the time. Merrill functioned as the representative agent for York in exchange for an enormous fee. It was their job to manage and oversee the sale process, which included interacting with prospective buyers.

The process of selling a large public company is time-consuming and labor-intensive. First, a prospectus had to be written and distributed to prospective buyers and the investment community. Then an endless series of detailed and repetitive meetings needed to be held with interested buyers and the countless analysts, bankers, investment firms, and legal entities that might participate in the deal. Over and over again, senior management reviewed past financial performance, future earnings projections, restructuring plans, product development activities, sales forecasts, customer contracts, and virtually every other aspect of the business.

Commercial banks, investment banks, ratings agencies, Wall Street analysts, and an endless stream of potential buyers were all standing in line to hear our story. On and on it went for many months. This was more than a full-time job; there was little time left to manage the business. That's the price that had to be paid so that a few people involved in the process could get very rich. The company's well-being and that of its workforce weren't important. The "deal" was everything. It's the American way, don't you know?

As representatives of the shareholders of York International, the York board of directors were obligated by law to sell the com-

"LET'S SEE A SHOW OF HANDS FOR AN L B O THAT COULD RUIN OUR COMPANY BUT MAKE US FILTHY RICH."

pany to the highest bidder they felt confident could secure the financing that would be required to close the deal. Determining the highest bidder was easy, but trying to ascertain whether the buyer could close the deal was much more difficult. Failure to close, for whatever reason, would have serious consequences for York. So one of Merrill Lynch's primary responsibilities was to advise the company on the likelihood that the buyer could secure financing.

As the selling process progressed, the number of serious potential buyers was reduced to the two strongest candidates: Snyder General Corporation and Citicorp Venture Capital. Snyder General was a major competitor in the heating, ventilating, air-conditioning, and refrigeration business, while Citicorp Venture Capital was an investment arm of Citicorp Bank. It soon became obvious that both of these companies desperately wanted to acquire York. As is typically the case when more than one prospective buyer shows strong competitive interest, an "auction" process was set up to extract the highest bid for the company.

The senior management representatives who were leading the Snyder and Citicorp teams were focused on determining what price their company should pay to buy York. Each prospective buyer knew that the other interested party was determined to be the winning bidder. With this as background, it is easy to understand why the projected future earnings of York that they forecast to support their bids were extraordinarily high. No matter how much tempering and cautioning I, and the York senior management team, attempted to convey to both prospective buyers, their forecasted numbers were overly optimistic. They knew that they couldn't justify the high price that their company would have to pay to win the bid unless York's future performance was exceptional. It was almost a reversal of roles: the seller advising caution and the buyer showing no restraint. Happy days!

The culmination of the bidding process took place over a weekend in a prominent hotel in New York City. Assembled were the York board of directors with their contingent of lawyers and advisers; the Merrill Lynch team with their lawyers and support staff; top executives, lawyers, and support staff from Snyder General and Citicorp; and economists and bankers of all shapes and sizes. Seemed like a cast of thousands. The Snyder and Citicorp entourages set up shop on different floors. The York entourage staked out a large meeting room on yet another floor. The show was about to begin.

The York group first heard a presentation from its chief legal counsel, who advised on the legal ramifications of the bidding process. The presentation was long but very interesting. The part that sticks in my head to this day dealt with the board's obligation to its shareholders to extract the highest price possible from the prospective buyers. It was also the board's responsibility to make their best determination of closing prospects, which meant factoring in the strength of buyer financing and the possibility of government antitrust restrictions if the purchase were deemed to be anticompetitive.

Perhaps the most telling part of the presentation was the lawyer's emphasis on the single-mindedness that was required in obtaining the highest purchase price without consideration of the company's or its employees' future prospects. For example, if one prospective buyer was prepared to expand the company and increase employment, it was not to receive preferential treatment over another prospective buyer that was planning to liquidate the business and terminate all employees. All that mattered were the best interests of the business owners, the shareholders. That was the law, and if the board failed in this regard they could, and likely would, be sued by a contingent of shareholders.

Following these preliminaries, both prospective buyers were separately invited into the room to make a presentation to the board. Each presentation began with an offer to purchase York at a certain price and with a commitment to close the transaction by a certain date. At great length, each party reviewed its expected sources of funding and how much equity it was prepared to invest in the deal. Once the York board heard the offered purchase price, they then focused on the evidence that each party presented as to the level of financial commitment that its prospective lenders had made to support the deal.

In the case of Snyder General, considerable discussion also took place regarding antitrust issues and the possibility that the government might delay or prohibit the purchase. Since Citicorp was not already in the same types of business that York was in, antitrust issues were not a problem for them.

When the initial presentations were finished, and both Snyder and Citicorp had returned to their meeting areas, a lengthy discussion took place with the board, Merrill Lynch, and numerous other parties who were acting as advisers on the deal. How strong was each party's opening bid? Was the level of equity that each bidder had committed sufficient to complete the deal? How firm did the prospective lenders' commitment to each bidder appear to be? Would there be antitrust issues with the government? Was it likely that the party with the lower bid would increase its offer once it was told it was the low bidder?

As expected, the board then asked Merrill Lynch, the agent that was representing York, to approach the low bidder to request that they increase their bid. When that was accomplished, Merrill returned to the board with the higher bid. Subsequently, another thorough discussion took place to review all of the questions that had been reviewed previously. Once again the board asked Merrill to approach the previous high bidder, which was now the low bidder, and ask them to raise their bid. This was shuttle diplomacy at its finest. The auction was under way but still a long way from its conclusion.

Round after round of this process took place throughout the night and the following day. No sleep; a few extended breaks; a single-minded focus: squeeze the bidders as hard as possible. Higher, higher, and higher; they weren't yet at their breaking point. Finally, after more than twenty-four hours of nonstop negotiations, it was apparent that the parties had reached their limit. Snyder General's final offer was $59.50 per share; Citicorp's final offer was $57.50 per share. The board would have to decide the winner.

The main questions were, could Snyder General come up with the financing to complete the deal, and what was the likelihood that the deal would escape government antitrust scrutiny? Was Citicorp more likely to complete the deal because their financing was more certain and there were no antitrust issues?

And the winner was...Citicorp.

Even though Citicorp's bid was lower, the board concluded that they were more likely to be able to close on the deal. Their financing commitments appeared to be firm, and there were no antitrust issues. As the corporate plane that I got on late Saturday night began to climb to its cruising altitude, I looked out the window on a clear night to see the moon in all its beauty. A rush of adrenaline followed and I thought to myself, it's finally over. I would make enough money from the deal to never need to work again. I had reached the pinnacle of my profession. I had seen much of the world. And I had experienced one of the highest levels of financial transactions in the business world. I was free at last, free at last; thank god I was free at last!

But the event turned out to be far from over. Citicorp's financing was not at all what the York board had been led to believe. In order to close the deal, it was necessary for the York management team to spend endless months and an enormous amount of energy in support of Citicorp's efforts to secure financing. And the level of equity that Citicorp was prepared to invest in the deal was a fraction of what the board had been told. So now a new round of endless nonproductive activities was about to begin. Meetings with commercial banks, investment banks, mezzanine lenders, ratings agencies, and other Wall Street institutions from the United States and Europe would soon be under way.

What should have taken two months to complete seemed to drag on forever. But finally the financing was in place and the closing date was set. Since I was president of York International, I was the person who was primarily responsible for signing the closing documents. I'm not exaggerating when I say that I signed hundreds of lengthy written documents, many of which weren't readable in a single lifetime. All I could do was hope that the lawyers got it right. My signing hand was seriously fatigued halfway through the ordeal. I wouldn't be surprised if I signed a confession to a capital crime without realizing it. Ridiculous; an absolute fucking waste of time. Doesn't anyone know that we've got a company to run?

But that's the way transactions are done. Any wonder companies can get so screwed up?

Perhaps the funniest part of the story came at the end of the process. Citicorp invested so little equity capital in the deal that after they extracted fees from York for the work they had done to secure financing for their own deal, it appeared that they had withdrawn far more than the amount of their original equity investment. In other words, it appeared that they bought the company without investing any of their own money: the ultimate in LBO deals. And the legal and professional fees were phenomenal. But that's how it was done; better get used to it.

When Citicorp took over the company, they made me an offer that they thought I couldn't refuse to stay on as president of the company. But I was so fatigued, so disappointed, and so angry with their handling of the acquisition that I rejected the offer and resigned instead. No one believed that I would walk away from my position, but I did…and never regretted it.

Chapter 15
Off to See the Wizard!

By early 1991 so much of life had already happened for me. As a kid I had subconsciously formulated a list of objectives, and it seemed like I had, more or less, attained them all: gotten a good education; married and raised a family; had a successful working career; attained financial independence; and traveled much of the world. And along the way I had experienced many of life's more notable experiences. Operas, plays, and concerts? Nothing new there. Baseball, football, hockey, and basketball playoffs? Had seen them all. Country clubs, fine restaurants, and world-class resorts were already old hat. I had started businesses, built homes, and learned how to enjoy a good book. How much more was there yet to do? How much more did I still want to do?

When I was just a kid playing football in the streets, my friends and I all had similar experiences; none of us had done much of anything up to that point. But by age forty-six I was in a place that many people would never get to in a lifetime. Certainly, my parents had never had many of my experiences. Ever been to the World Series, Dad? No, but I've listened to it on the radio many times. Ever been to Saudi Arabia? No, but I can find it on a map. Ever think about joining that country club on the other side of town? No, but I was invited to a luncheon there once. Do you know what, Dad? I'm not sure that any of that stuff really matters. I used to think it did, but now I'm not so sure.

That uncertainty was foremost in my mind one early spring afternoon in 1991 as I was sitting on the deck of the beautiful home we had built in Bristol, Tennessee. Elaine had come out of the house to hand me the phone; Jack W from Beacon Capital was on the phone, asking to speak to me.

Hello, Jack…

As it turned out, Beacon Capital was a leveraged buyout firm that one year earlier had purchased the heating and air-conditioning division of the Coleman Company in Wichita, Kansas. That acquisition had not gone well in its first year of ownership under Beacon. In fact, they were having a difficult time servicing the large debt that had been incurred as a result of the highly leveraged purchase.

Sounds familiar, doesn't it?

Jack had called to ask if I might be interested in joining the company that Beacon had purchased and had renamed Evcon Industries. He explained that he had been given my name by several people in the HVAC industry. Would I be willing to come to Toronto, Canada, to talk about the possibility of heading up Evcon Industries as CEO and chairman of the board of directors? Beacon would offer a very substantial equity position in the company and I would have a free hand in running the business.

Evcon was a significant player in the HVAC industry but nowhere near the size of York International, the company that I had headed up just prior to my retirement. It was true that the size of the equity grant that Beacon was offering made the deal very attractive, but the Evcon job wasn't as prestigious as the York position. I was retired; I liked Bristol, Tennessee; I didn't need to work anymore.

I was lost; I was melancholy; my business ventures were struggling. Sure, I'll fly out to talk with you, Jack.

I had never heard so much complaining in my life. Elaine couldn't understand why I would consider the Evcon job. There

was no way she wanted to move to Wichita, Kansas. No way! She was having none of that Wizard of Oz business. So when I finally decided to try out this new adventure, she had to be dragged all the way to Kansas. Things only got worse when I unilaterally decided to buy a much smaller home in Wichita than the one we had built in Bristol. It was in a great neighborhood, and the back yard bordered on the grounds of the private school that Dan would be attending. More importantly, the home was vacant and immediately available. What's not to like?

The fact of the matter was that I wasn't at all sure that this new venture was for me. I didn't know if any of this was going to work out, but I decided to give it a try. If I didn't like it, I would be on the next flight back to Bristol. For that reason, we decided to hold on to the Bristol home just in case.

I wasn't in the mood to put up with any crap from Beacon Capital. Prior to accepting the Evcon position, I sat across from the Beacon management team and the principal investors in Beacon and told them they should retract their offer if their interpersonal business style was going to be any different from the pleasant face they showed during the getting-to-know-you process. I made it perfectly clear that I would resign immediately if things between us didn't go smoothly. Fortunately, they were always great to work with. I'm sure that was because Evcon turned out to be a highly successful company. It would have been very different if the business had not done so well.

The first day on the Evcon job everything went smoothly. The guy I was replacing impressed me in several ways, so I offered him an opportunity to stay with the company in an advisory role, reporting directly to me. That worked for quite a while but in the end I concluded that I had to terminate his position. That was especially hard to do because he was a first-class citizen and he had given the job everything he had. When the day came that I had to tell him that his employment was being terminated, I walked into his office and closed the door behind me. He looked up at me and before I could say a word he said, "Oh no!" He knew what was about to happen. You can't imagine how hard that was for me to do or how truly saddened I was over the whole thing.

But I am always quick to say that whenever I've had to terminate someone, the burden that is placed on the recipient is far greater than what I ever had to experience.

"Oh no!" Very sad words.

One of the problems that I had to face when I started at Evcon was a union organizing drive that was in its final stages. I really didn't have much time to convince the workforce that we should remain union free. Less than two weeks after I started, the vote was held and the union won with a plurality of one vote. After the election the company filed an objection with the National Labor Relations Board over union conduct on the day of the election. As it turned out, on the morning of the vote the union handed out lists of signatures to all employees as they entered the parking lot under page headings that said *We are all voting for the union.* The fact was that employees whose signatures were on the pages had originally signed a page that had said *I have received a hat and/or T-shirt from the union.* During the union organizing drive any employees who accepted a hat or T-shirt from the union had to acknowledge receipt with their signature. The new heading, *We are all voting for the union,* appeared to have been glued to the top of the page at a later date. Surely that deception cost the company far more than the one-vote margin of defeat, but the NLRB didn't see it our way. Evcon would henceforth be represented by the International Association of Machinists.

Although the IAM was often characterized as a difficult union to deal with, their relationship with Evcon generally turned out to be favorable. As was almost always the case, however, restrictive "work rules" were one of the biggest problems that we faced. Employees were frequently prohibited from doing jobs that were outside the relatively narrow scope of their job description. So when work was slow in one area of production, it was often not possible to ask them to work in another area of the plant where they were needed. And any attempt to terminate a union employee, for almost any reason, was virtually impossible. In effect, once new employees passed their probationary period we likely had them for life. Kind of like tenure at a university. But we seemed to be able to make things work. In fact, having a union contract meant that we didn't have to bend over backwards every time some trivial problem happened on the shop floor. Just get out the union contract and follow what it said to resolve the problem.

The issues facing Evcon were classic: virtually every department in the company needed fixing to one degree or another. Many of the key managers were not up to the job of leading their operation in a new direction. The first thing that had to be done was replace the heads of manufacturing, materials, finance, and sales and marketing. The heads of engineering and human resources were survivors who were able to fully integrate themselves into the management team. When everyone was in place I stood back and realized that we had put together an absolutely kick-ass team. There was nothing that we couldn't do. Evcon charged onto the scene, seemingly from out of nowhere.

There were no simple solutions to fixing this company; everything that we did followed the back-to-basics philosophy. If we concentrated on building everything from the ground up, on a solid foundation, we knew we would have a company that would thrive in an industry that often seemed to lack direction and good leadership. No Harvard MBA required. No high-priced consultants brought on board to wave a magic wand over everything and then disappear into the sunset. No management by edict or one-liners. We built from the bottom up using all the best materials. And the results would exceed everyone's expectations, except my own.

We would do it all.

Manufacturing was changed from the so-called "batch" process to "just in time." This allowed us to build only the product we could sell immediately; no more building months worth of inventory and then putting it in storage until it was sold. The price that had to be paid for all this streamlining was the far more frequent change of production setups in manufacturing, but working inventory and finished goods inventory fell to extremely low levels. The amount of paperwork that was required to manage the shop floor fell from daily stacks that filled a desktop to virtually nothing at all, because "paperless shop floor control" relied on visual cues to initiate operations in manufacturing and materials. Conversion to "just in time" and "paperless shop floor control" was a major undertaking but one that was well worth the effort: our production capacity soared as our manufacturing costs plummeted.

Because our new vice president of sales and marketing had a broad background in our industry, he was able to generate an extensive base of distributors and dealers who were interested in our product. He knew the potential customer base and our potential customers knew him; as a result, sales and profit margins increased dramatically. There were many times that production just couldn't keep up with demand. And when we sold more, our cost of manufacturing dropped because of increased efficiency that came with greater manufacturing volume. That cycle kept repeating itself as we moved forward.

Similar improvements were made in the materials area. Because we had changed to the "just in time" method of production, all of the items that we purchased from our suppliers had to be ordered correctly and received in a timely manner. If we got it wrong, production would grind to a halt because there was no backup stock in our facility. However, because there were no surplus materials in the warehouse, the transportation of components within the facility was highly efficient and storage costs were minimal.

And as production volume increased, we were able to negotiate much more favorable pricing from our suppliers. Lower material costs, of course, allowed us to sell our product at lower prices while often simultaneously increasing profit margins. Once again we created a cycle that kept repeating itself as our business grew.

In every business that I have ever managed I have always put new product development at the top of the priority list. It stands to reason that if you want customers to buy more of your product and less of the competition's, you must offer them something that performs better and hopefully costs less than the competition's. It's an unbeatable combination, if you can do it.

Evcon was no exception. New product development was number one on the list of priorities. From top to bottom, the entire line of air conditioners, heat pumps, air handlers, coils, and furnaces were redesigned to be more efficient, more reliable, quieter, smaller, and less costly than the competition's. It took a great deal of time and money, but in the end we had elbowed our way to a competitive position in the industry. Sales increased dramatically while profit margins soared.

I said that new product development was first on our list of priorities, but of almost equal importance was employee relations. In fact, for the company to reach its full potential, improvements needed to be made simultaneously in every area, not just one or two: manufacturing, materials, sales and marketing, product development, and employee relations. This broad-based approach was the foundation that future success would be built on. But employee relations is an area that is often neglected by senior management. In fact, because it is difficult to measure directly, the benefits of increasing employee morale may not be considered an area of priority within a company.

Good employee relations start with good communications. The workforce must understand where the company is headed and why. To this end, numerous two-way communications methods were established, including: all-employee meetings, small-group meetings, open-door policies, mentoring programs, and the frequent presence of top management on the shop floor.

Courtesy, fairness, respect, dignity, and honesty were not just emphasized but were the subjects of numerous employee communications meetings. We couldn't just blindly expect employees to practice these things; we had to talk about them at length and pro-

"*Perhaps we could find a way to redefine 'profit.'*"

mote them in every way we could. The message to the employees was, "You matter, and this company will do everything possible to make your work life as good as it can possibly be."

So much effort, so much change, so much progress. Evcon had gained a strong foothold in the HVAC industry. So what was next?

Sell the company.

That was not a surprise to me; that was always the plan, and I knew it. York International, the company that I had previously headed up, the company that had bought Bristol Compressors, was knocking on the door. They wanted to buy Evcon.

It took a few months of negotiation, but in the end a deal was reached. Evcon joined the York family and at the end of 1994 I retired for the second time. Beacon Capital and I had made a bundle of money. Evcon's employees were in great shape and we had left the company in far better condition than we had found it.

In 2003, several years after the death of the Beacon CEO, Jack Whitely, his wife, Eleanor, published Jack's unfinished memoir, titled *Memories (Some Amusing, I Hope)*. On page 276, Jack paid me a compliment that I believe beautifully summarizes the relationship that I had with everyone at Beacon Capital and Evcon Industries:

"Mike Young was one of the most capable businessmen I had ever met, certainly the most capable I had ever worked with. He was very smart, had great capacity, had strong leadership abilities and, into the bargain, had a congenial personality and great sense of humor. Within a few months, he strengthened the management, streamlined our product lines and improved our production efficiency. It became clear that he was going to turn the company around."

Chapter 16
Don't Answer It, You Fool

The Evcon experience had ended with great success, but that was now behind me. The home that Elaine and I built in Tennessee had been sold midway through the Evcon undertaking, so there was nothing in Bristol to go back to. We were then living in a larger home in Wichita that we had completely remodeled. Elaine was happy with the new home, but not with much else. We had also recently purchased a 360-acre parcel of land a few miles outside the Wichita city limits. On that land we had built two modest homes, one for my son Alex and his family, and a small getaway home for Elaine and me. Actually, the truth of the matter was that the getaway home was more for me than it was for Elaine. One bedroom, one bath, living room, small kitchen, enclosed porch, and a five-car garage.

I had set out to make the 360 acres the most beautiful land in the area. Trimming trees, clearing debris, building ponds, erecting perimeter fences, and planting grass was pretty much a full-time job. The little additional time that I did have was frequently devoted to the hands-on projects that I had always enjoyed doing.

There's not much reason to have a getaway home if you don't get away, is there? So it wasn't long until Elaine and I had separated, I was living in the getaway home, and we had begun divorce proceedings. But that's a whole story in and of itself, so suffice it to say that after an extraordinarily difficult divorce I was in every way possible unattached, uncommitted, and unobligated. There was nothing more that I needed or wanted except for everyone to get out of my way and leave me alone. I was free and I was never, ever going back.

Or so I thought.

Ring…ring…ring…

Don't answer it, you fool…don't answer it…I warned you…

Hello…oh hi, Bob, how are you?

It was Robert P, then CEO and chairman of the board of York International.

Yeah, Bob, I'm just out here goofing off in Kansas; I'm leaving it up to the rest of you guys to save the world…sure, Bob, if there's ever anything that I can do to help you, just ask…

Bob was asking if I would temporarily take on a consulting role with York International. The Bristol division of York, the business that I had once managed, had recently purchased half ownership in a company called Scroll Technologies in Arkadelphia, Arkansas. The business was jointly owned with the Carrier Corporation, a major competitor of York. Scroll compressors were a relatively new technology that posed a major threat to the reciprocating compressors that had always been produced at the Bristol, Tennessee, facility. The joint venture with Carrier was not going well. Would I represent York on a short-term basis at the Arkadelphia facility to help resolve numerous operating problems?

Once again the timing was right. The divorce proceedings were driving me nuts and any chance to temporarily get out of the Wichita area would have a positive impact on that situation. Okay, Bob, I'll do it, but just on a short-term basis. When do you want me to start? That soon, eh?

I soon found out that the Carrier Corporation, the single largest producer of heating, ventilating, air-conditioning, and refrigeration products in the world, and York's largest competitor, had a bunch of absolute idiots overseeing its Scroll Technologies joint venture. If there was a stronger way to say it, I would have used different words. If they were representative of the rest of the Carrier management team, I didn't know how they stayed in business, let alone how they had become such a dominant factor in the industry. But I couldn't fire them all, so I had to find a way to put up with their incompetence. That may have been the single most difficult thing that I *ever* had to do in business; no exaggeration.

There were so many things wrong with the Scroll Tech business that it was difficult to decide where to start. Manufacturing operations had problems everywhere you looked, quality control was pitiful, and the sales and marketing function was basically nonexistent. But upon closer examination it became apparent that many of the operational problems that existed in manufacturing and quality control were the result of numerous deficiencies in the design of the compressor product line. Because of these design problems, it was virtually impossible to produce a high-quality product efficiently. And because the product was so poorly designed, and so costly, it was not possible for the sales and marketing department to sell the product outside the captive Carrier and York divisions, which were obligated to buy from their sister company, Scroll Tech.

There were relatively straightforward solutions to many of the design problems, but Carrier, and to a lesser extent York itself, just couldn't see the obvious. There was resistance to virtually every change that had to be made. For that reason, I was forced to work independently with several outstanding engineers in product development, most notably Joe H, to create what later came to be called the "next generation" product. Carrier fought it all the way, but this new compressor line turned out to be more efficient, smaller, quieter, less costly, more reliable, and far easier to produce than the product that was then in production. But, because of the complete resistance to change that was prevalent throughout the company, it took several years for Scroll Tech to fully implement all of the production changes that were required. Unfortunately, it didn't take Scroll Tech's competitors long to copy many of the most important of those changes.

I wasn't able to continue working directly with Scroll Tech for very long. As it turns out, York International was having difficulty with its main Bristol Compressor business and they asked me if I would be willing to temporarily return as president, CEO, and chairman of Bristol Compressors, reporting to Robert P, the CEO of York. I loved Bristol Compressors and I felt obligated to try to help it get back on track, so I agreed. Robert P had reported to me when I was president and COO of York; now the roles would be reversed.

It was the end of 1995. I was back in Bristol, living in the same subdivision where Elaine and I had once lived, but this time I was with Frankie, a girlfriend I had met in Wichita. We were heading off on what I fully expected to be a short-term commitment.

Joe L, the CEO of Bristol whom I was replacing, had succeeded me when I first left Bristol to take the York International position. For the most part, he had done a good job heading up Bristol, but buying into the Scroll Tech joint venture had clearly been a major mistake. To make things worse, Bristol had opened another manufacturing facility in Sparta, North Carolina. Major financial losses at Scroll Tech and Sparta, and the dilution of management efforts among the Virginia, Arkansas, and North Carolina facilities were taking a heavy toll on the business. I wanted to keep Joe on the team so I asked if he would return to running the engineering and quality control functions at Bristol, which is what he had done prior to succeeding me.

One of Bristol Compressor's greatest strengths had always been its highly efficient operation, which was made possible in part because Bristol did not have numerous facilities located throughout the country. Apparently, Joe L, Robert P, and the York board of directors didn't appreciate how important that fact was. The problems that Bristol had created for itself when it expanded into Arkansas and North Carolina were difficult to undo.

As I look back on it now, it occurs to me that the expansion of facilities might well have been brought on by a fear that Bristol, because of its size, was likely to become the target of a union organizing drive. As the thinking sometimes goes, employees are less likely to seek a union if they are concerned that production could be relocated to another facility. Flawed thinking; far better to keep employees happy in their jobs so they don't want or need a union. But opening up new facilities wouldn't discourage a union organizing attempt. Just before my arrival back in Bristol, a union organizing drive had been initiated, as had happened at Evcon when I first arrived. Early indications were that the union was in a strong position and was likely to win.

When I was first at Bristol I had established a good rapport with the workforce: I had gained their respect, and they knew I genuinely cared about them and would always look out for their best interests. Those feelings had continued after I left Bristol to run York, and when I returned, there was an overwhelming show of support. The endless days and nights that I had spent on the shop floor, and the countless employee meetings that I had held had paid off. When the election ballots were counted, the National Labor Relations Board, which supervised the election, informed us that the company had defeated the union by the largest margin of victory of any company that fell into their categorization of large corporations. Enough said.

I wasn't counting the days, but I had every intention of finding a permanent replacement for myself and heading back to Wichita before long. One year, perhaps two? Who knew, but I never would have guessed that it would be four years before that happened. I was then at the beginning of my second Bristol commitment, and it was obvious that there was a lot that had to be done. Every operation in the company would need to be thoroughly addressed with a back-to-basics approach: manufacturing, materials, quality, finance, sales and marketing, human resources, and, most importantly, new product development. High on the list of priorities was figuring out what to do with Bristol's two newest facilities.

So much money and effort had been spent building, equipping, and staffing Sparta, but it had turned out to be nothing more than a millstone around Bristol's neck. Since the facility had virtually no resale value, a little more than a year after I arrived back at Bristol, we closed the doors and took a huge write-off. It had to be done.

The Scroll Tech operation was another story. The complex relationship between Bristol and Carrier made exiting the business difficult. When Bristol originally bought into the venture, it did so partly to protect the reciprocating compressor business that it already had with Carrier's residential air-conditioning division. A split with Carrier over Scroll Tech would certainly lead to the loss of that business. Long-term contracts between the companies obligated Bristol to continue the Scroll Tech joint venture or risk legal problems.

That wasn't Bristol's only problem. Scroll compressors were emerging as a major factor in the HVAC industry. Bristol's largest

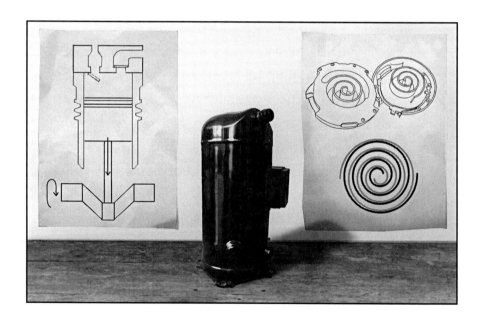

competitor, Copeland, had made a full commitment to this new technology because they wanted to move the industry away from reciprocating compressors where Bristol was so strong. As a division of Emerson Electric Corporation, they had extraordinarily deep pockets and were ready, willing, and able to spend whatever it took to change the industry. Pursuing new technology is an admirable objective, but scroll compressors were not in Bristol's best interests. The cost to follow in the scroll direction would have been prohibitive.

In spite of that fact, Bristol had thought that it needed to get on the scroll bandwagon. That was the primary reason they entered into the joint venture with Carrier. But the results had been predictable: Scroll Tech was a bottomless pit that Bristol had jumped into. The answer to the scroll threat wasn't to follow Copeland; Bristol needed to take a different approach. It needed products that were superior to the scroll but could be built with the manufacturing capability that already existed at the Bristol, Virginia, facility. That wasn't an easy thing to do, but it had to be done.

While all this was going on, Frankie and I decided to get married. I'm not sure what happened to the unattached, uncommitted, and unobligated idea, but whatever it was, it was all out the window then. I was working, I was married, and I was…kind of happy. But as I look back on it now, I don't think Frankie and I were ever head-over-heels in love. It seems like we were just good friends. We had fun together even though we were different in so many ways. But about three years later, when we were together on a business trip to Asia, Frankie told me she didn't like business traveling and hated the business socializing she had been asked to do on the trip. It was then I sensed that the marriage would soon be over.

But that end was still a way off, so *my full attention* was then *focused on* fixing the Bristol *business*. (After writing those few words I was tempted to go back and erase them but they actually say a lot about my marriage.) Anyway, the thing Bristol most needed to do was develop breakthrough products that would outperform the scroll and would be producible with the equipment already in the Bristol plant.

Bristol had a number of good engineers, but one in particular was exceptionally creative. Joe H had the ability to see things that few other engineers could see. He and I were alike in that way, so we were always able to work through ideas that would frequently go way over the heads of others. One day Joe H came to me with an idea that had never entered my mind before. He had started thinking about how a compressor's output could be cycled to half capacity whenever the air-conditioning system did not need to be operating at full capacity. The ability to operate the compressor at either full or half capacity would allow the system in which it was installed to operate far more efficiently.

As Joe and I began talking the basic idea through, we suddenly realized that there was an ingenious mechanism that could relatively easily be incorporated in our current product line to accomplish our objective. We were on the verge of a major breakthrough, something that was truly revolutionary. The idea was so simple that we were able to build the first rudimentary hardware to illustrate the concept in just a few hours. I've still got that first hardware in my home office. It wasn't long after that the Twin Single, or TS compressor went into production.

Several years after the compressor had entered production, and after I had left Bristol for the second time, I was told by the president of Copeland, Bristol's largest competitor, that the TS compressor had terrified them when the product first entered the market. Unfortunately, it never was able to displace the scroll, but that limitation was caused by internal shortcomings at Bristol, not anything to do with the compressor itself. To this day it stands as an idea that has yet to reach its full potential.

The TS compressor was not the only technological break-through that was made during my second round at Bristol Compressors. When I returned, I asked the engineering depart-ment to radically rethink how our compressor products were designed. I challenged them to examine every part in the com-pressor closely. Why was that part needed? Could it be removed, simplified, made smaller or less costly? Could it be combined with some other component, or functionally replace something else in the compressor?

As expected, Joe H was the visionary. It wasn't long before he was able to demonstrate a compressor that had remarkably high efficiency, was half the size, had 40 percent fewer parts, and was approximately 40 percent lower in cost than the products we were then producing. But in the initial stages of development the compressor was not as quiet as competing products, so it was clear that a major commitment of additional engineering resources would still be required. This was a topic of great debate. To my regret, the project was displaced by a far less advanced product that was considered by some members of the leadership team to be a "safer" alternative. The breakthrough compressor, which came to be known as the M-4, was a good news/bad news story. The good news was that the compressor could have been a game changer; the bad news was that it never entered production. The reason had everything to do with a failure of leadership, not a failure of technology. That failure of leadership was my own. I should have insisted that a commitment be made to resolve the sound problem, but I didn't.

My time at Bristol was again coming to an end. I had informed the York board that after four years on the job, I was planning to retire once again. The job that I originally thought would take one or two years had lasted far longer than I had expected. I had no regrets; I just needed to do something different.

Then came surprising news from the board. Robert P was unexpectedly fired, and John T, York's president and chief operating officer, had been named the new CEO. John T and the board asked me to delay my retirement and to take on responsibility for York's Unitary Products Division, in addition to the Bristol Division. Pitch in and help us out was the request. I didn't really want to do that, and I didn't really like John T, but I did it anyway.

No one realized at the time just how short-term a commitment it was going to be. John T almost immediately got himself in serious trouble with the board. As a board member myself, I knew about the trouble that John was in even though the board had excluded me from subsequent meetings on the subject because I was also a member of management. It's a long and interesting story, but I'll get to the heart of the matter. John T was fired for cause, and the York board then asked me if I would succeed him as CEO. Bristol...York...Evcon...Bristol...York again?

Why not?

Chapter 17
Homecoming

John T, the CEO successor to Robert P, had hardly had a chance to move into Bob's old office before the board threw him out too. It was just a matter of months before his shenanigans caught up with him. This CEO business sure does put you in the crosshairs! And now York was asking me again if I would lead the company.

Listen, fellas, I've been telling you over and over again that I'm going to retire and drift off into the sunset…

But that need to constantly prove myself to myself was still there. Good enough was really never good enough; there was always something more that had to be done. Perhaps that's the telltale sign of an inferiority complex, I don't know. But what I did know was that I had to do the York thing one more time. Four years and I'd be gone; there would be no encore.

So Frankie and I made a U-turn on our way from Bristol back to Wichita; York was our new destination. Took us only two days of looking to find a beautiful condominium home that was only a stone's throw away from the York facility. Since my contractual arrangement with York required that they provide me a home with expenses paid in York, I was able to transition with a minimum of complication. Frankie was in charge of decorating; all I had to do was show up after work.

The pattern of my life tended to repeat itself. We lived in York while simultaneously maintaining the home we had just refurbished in Wichita. If things went bad at York International, I would be out of there in no time flat.

I've always tried to keep everything as simple as possible, and this new endeavor would be no exception. All I needed to get started at York was to lighten up Bob's/John's old office on a self-imposed budget of a couple thousand dollars. Never could understand how some guys could spend hundreds of thousands of dollars on their offices. The first thing I had to do was get the heavy red drapes off the windows and then get rid of the monstrous sofa that looked like something grandma used to own. The office was sure different from the way it had been when I was last there, but I had it back in shape in a couple of days.

Yeah, in some ways I felt like I had just come home after an extended journey. But in many other ways things were very different. For one thing, the board was, to a man, different from the last York board that I knew. In fact, I really didn't know any of the guys, other than through the encounters that I'd had after returning to Bristol and during the brief John T CEO period when I had been invited to rejoin the board.

York International Corporation Board of Directors, 2001

But all was not well on the home front. The U-turn that Frankie and I had made on our way back to Wichita hadn't pleased her at all. I had promised to take her home after what we thought would be a relatively short stay in Bristol, but that plan was now out the window. Wasn't long before she had her bags packed and was back in Wichita, ostensibly for an indefinite period. Of course by that point the end of the marriage was clearly in sight. Fortunately, there was no real animosity between us, and the end was uneventful. Her continuing friendship is still important to me to this day.

I had always relied on internal growth, not acquisitions, to expand the businesses that I had managed in the past. But in the eleven years since I had last been president, York had grown, in large part by acquiring other companies. Growth through acquisition is the easy, but costly and risky, way of growing a business. It took a lot more talent and a lot more work to systemically grow a business, but the end product was often far better.

Some of the acquisitions that York had made over the years were beneficial, Bristol and Evcon being notable examples. Many others were ill-advised and ended up costing the company dearly. Many of the businesses that had been acquired were redundant with other business segments that York already had. Certain other acquisitions did not perform financially as expected, or required excess management attention because of unforeseen weaknesses in the business. My first objective, therefore, was to straighten out the organizational mess that had overtaken the company.

Reorganizing major segments of the company was a difficult and unpleasant task for numerous reasons. First and foremost, it required closing and consolidating some of the company's largest manufacturing and administrative facilities. Employees at those locations would be out of a job through no fault of their own. For a company that prided itself on the well-being of its employees, that was difficult to reconcile, but it had to be done if York was to thrive in the future.

Whenever a facility was closed, the "book value" of the asset, as well as the costs associated with employee severance, obsolete inventory, and the relocation of capital equipment, had to be written off against current earnings. The financial community, which closely monitors the earnings performance of all public companies, needed to be constantly reminded that current earnings were being penalized to improve future financial performance. In a world where almost everyone is focused on short-term performance, that was a lot to ask.

Every step in the multifaceted reorganizational process had to be explained to the financial community when it was initiated: why was it necessary, how much would it cost, and what future benefit would it bring? To an outside observer it must have appeared to be a never-ending process. Many of the initiatives brought negative attention to the York board because they had been the ones who approved the original acquisition of the business. It always begged the question "Why did you guys buy this thing in the first place?" It wasn't much fun dealing with a board who constantly had to explain themselves to the financial community.

How difficult it was to tell employees that their facility was going to be closed and they were going to be out of a job. But I always insisted that the president of the division that was closing a particular facility be the one to convey the bad news personally. In one instance, however, the president of the largest facility that we ever closed was sidetracked at the last minute and was unable to deliver the bad news himself. That left the job up to me since time did not allow us to delay the announcement; the rumor mill would have immediately spread the word if we did not.

Many hundreds of employees in countless meetings sat in front of me. Some women, some old folks, lots of tough guys. We had six plainclothes tough guys of our own in every meeting. But if there was a riot, I'm not sure how much good they would have been. At each meeting I said the same thing over and over again: The facility was losing money because it was significantly underutilized. The products they produced were near duplicates of those being produced at two other locations. It was necessary that we close their facility.

They would drive home that day in their beat-up Pintos.

I would fly home on the company jet.

They would receive three months severance pay.

I would continue to receive my obscene paycheck.

They weren't sure they could continue to make their house payments.

My home was provided free of charge.

Sure seemed like something was wrong there. I didn't like it, but that's how it was.

The reorganization had clearly gotten off to a good start, as did most of the other initiatives that had been undertaken. Stand back, everyone, we're really starting to kick some ass. Then it happened; some fuck decided to fly a couple of airplanes into the World Trade Center complex. As the buildings collapsed, so did many parts of York's business. Gone in a flash. New building construction around the world came to a screeching halt.

York equipment had been used to air-condition and move conditioned air through the World Trade Center buildings. York equipment was in the Empire State Building, the Chicago Towers, the Sydney Opera House, the English/French Chunnel, and thousands of other major structures throughout the world. Would anything like them ever be built again? Would the world economy collapse into a major depression? You can hardly imagine the magnitude of the problem that faced us.

There was only one thing to do: try to claw our way back to the top. It was a difficult, lengthy, and uncertain process, but we got started. Year by year we made progress, but it is an absolute certainty that an enormous price had been paid. Things improved, but they were never as good as they otherwise would have been.

My previous CEO experiences had exposed me to many challenging and rewarding learning experiences: finance, banking, mergers and acquisitions, leveraged buyouts, board leadership, and so on. No one was ever born with those experiences. Every one of them had to be learned the old-fashioned way: through hard work and the constant cycle of success and failure. Little by little you learned; then one day you realized that you had gotten pretty good at it.

Up to that point, most of my executive experience had been with companies that were not publicly owned, so I had not been required to deal with the financial analysis community or ratings agencies, whose job it was to issue reports on the public companies they followed. Private companies do not have to report the details of their company's financial performance to the public; public companies do.

Report good quarterly numbers and life is good, the stock price may go up, and you probably get to keep your job a while longer.

When I ran York the first time I had been president and chief operating officer; public reporting at that time was one of the responsibilities of York's CEO. As president and COO, I oversaw the company's operations and didn't have to deal with the characters on Wall Street. That all changed when I returned to York as CEO.

At the end of every quarter it was my job to initiate an earnings conference call to all York shareholders who wished to participate, as well as the enormous community of financial analysts, banking interests, economists, and ratings agencies that followed our company. Everyone listened to every word that was spoken, and then the call was opened up for questions. You never knew what would be asked, but you had better know the answers. Make one mistake, or stumble in any way, and you would turn the dogs loose. The preparation that was required prior to these meetings took several days, but it was the stress that you felt that brought on total exhaustion. Fortunately, none of the conference calls ever went bad: there were no gaffes, and no major mistakes were made. So many things could have gone wrong; that they didn't surprises me to this day.

Quarterly conference calls were just one of many regular reporting activities. Analysts' meetings, bankers' meetings, shareholders' meetings, the list goes on and on. Every one required significant preparation and every one was stressful. You just couldn't make a major mistake: no way, no how!

One final note on the subject of reporting activities: Once every year, York and many other companies were invited to something called an "Electrical Products" analysts' meeting. Sitting in a large auditorium were hundreds of analysts who wanted to hear all about the dozens of companies that fell into their area of expertise. One after another the CEOs of the companies would make a presentation to the group and then open the floor to questions. Some of the analysts were fairly easy to deal with; others could be a little difficult; a few could be real assholes.

Pity the CEO who had poor earnings performance to report, or who had a bad story to tell. Some of them were really put upon at times. The funny part of the story, however, is that York International's presentation always followed that of General Electric. We never knew why things were ordered that way, but year after year that's the way it was. I invariably followed the presentation that was made by Jack Welch, the highly successful, highly regarded, and extraordinarily powerful CEO of General Electric. Man, he was a tough act to follow for many reasons, not the least of which is that he didn't take any shit from anyone. If he got a critical question, he would turn it around and stick it right up the questioner's ass. I, and every other presenter, always wished we were strong enough to do the same thing.

Life was moving merrily along on most fronts when suddenly, and almost simultaneously, a whole bunch of CEOs were caught with their hands in the cookie jar: Kenneth Lay, Jeff Skilling, Dennis Kozlowski, Bernie Ebbers, the list went on and on. For the first time, *CEO* became a household term, one with generally negative connotations. But hold on there, folks, we didn't all cook the books or buy six-thousand-dollar shower curtains. The spotlight was shining on everyone, and everyone was going to have to pay the price. From now on you CEOs and you board members are going to have to spend most of your time proving that you're not guilty of something or other, we're not even sure what.

The Sarbanes-Oxley regulation was just the start. Going forward, senior management and directors would have to spend an enormous amount of their time trying to ensure that they wouldn't end up penniless and behind bars. Some board members resigned their positions; other board members stopped focusing on the growth aspects of the business and thought only about financial reporting and auditing. The world of business had taken a sharp and ill-advised turn. We've got to all cover our asses, boys, no time to run a business.

York International, like almost every other company, got caught up in the malaise. Board meetings turned into two days of audit meetings. There was hardly any discussion of new product development, improved manufacturing methods, vendor agreements, sales contracts, or anything else that had to do with running the business. All we did was micromanage the books to ensure compliance.

Compliance had never been an issue, and would never be an issue. We had never needed close scrutiny to follow the rules. There was never any question about how we kept the books. But the misdeeds of a few would cause untold aggravation for the many. Running the business wasn't fun any longer. I would look back on my workday and realize that more than 80 percent of it had been wasted on accounting-related matters. It was time to start putting transition plans in place. I informed the board that I would be gone in a year; it was time to start looking for my replacement.

The person I recommended as my successor was a well-qualified internal candidate who had the full support of the board. My last year as a lame duck CEO was difficult. In deference to my likely successor's goals, I found myself in a position of compromise and concession. Next time I'll wait until the last minute to announce my retirement.

What the fuck? What next time?

Chapter 18
Autre

Different: I was always that way. When the other kids turned left, I turned right. There wasn't much that I disliked more than following the leader. Trailing along like an imprinted duck never worked for me. My entire life followed that pattern: I always saw things differently. Seemed like there was always another way; I just needed to find it.

Mom and Dad didn't understand that *need* to be different, and no one else did either. So it was never easy: Dad—conflict; Mom—conflict; friends—conflict; teachers—conflict; authority figures—conflict. Wasn't sure how I was ever going to get through life.

One thing was clear early on: if I didn't want to play follow the leader, I would have to learn to be less dependent on the things, the people, and the traditions that surrounded me. Dependency, it seemed, was the precursor to the status quo. That's what was keeping everyone in line, thinking the same way, and following the leader.

An entire life spent asking "why?" Why do we do it that way? In fact, why are we doing it at all? Isn't there a better, simpler, less complicated way? Hasn't anyone ever tried doing it this other way?

I must have been somewhere around eleven years old. One of the few "luxuries" our family had at that time was a Decca console stereo record player that sat at the far end of our combination living room/dining room. The only trouble with that arrangement was that the stereo was positioned far from the main seating area, which was the place to be if you wanted to listen to music.

The stereo had two portable speakers that slid out from a bottom shelf, but the speaker wires were short and didn't reach across the room. That wasn't much help at all. And Dad insisted that there was no other place in the room to relocate the stereo itself. No way to make those speaker wires longer, either, Dad said, and besides that people would just trip over them if they ran across the carpet.

I really didn't have any idea what I was doing, but I decided that I'd try something different anyway.

Looked like each of those speaker wires was double stranded. Maybe I could take some of the surplus wire that I found in the basement and connect it to the existing wires by cutting, stripping, twisting, and taping at different connecting points. Then I could drill holes through the floor near the baseboards to feed the wire under the floor, across the basement ceiling, and through another set of holes on the seating side of the room.

I sure wish I knew more about how homes were constructed so that I wouldn't mess something up in the basement. And I wasn't sure if just cutting and joining the wires together was the right thing to do. Dad and Mom would be mad if I screwed things up, or if I broke the stereo. Had to hurry, they were going to be back in a few hours.

Wow, it sounded great. I knew it would be better with the speakers on the other side of the room. Sure am glad that it worked, and that I decided to try something different.

Seemed like I always had an overabundance of new ideas. Not always great or even good ideas, but new ideas nonetheless. No apologies for the bad ideas, though. You can't expect a kid, or anyone else for that matter, to always have it figured out. The important thing was that I wasn't afraid to challenge the way things were being done. If someone hadn't questioned the status quo, we'd still be watching black-and-white TVs whose pictures constantly rolled because the "vertical hold" control didn't work right. Then again, some of you may be too young to appreciate that that once was a problem.

I never liked getting out of bed to turn the lights on or off in the bedroom that Gordy and I shared as kids. One day I decided to run two strings from the post of my bed to the light switch on the other side of our room. One of the strings ran over a nail that I drove into the wall, directly over the light switch, and was tied to the switch toggle with the aid of a notch that I made with a hacksaw blade. The second string attached in a similar manner around a second nail that was below the switch. When I pulled one string from my bed, the switch flipped up; when I pulled the other, it flipped down. It worked well enough, but Gordy never realized how brilliant the idea really was. Come on, Gordy, give me a break: it works, doesn't it?

Homework, and Detroit top forties radio: that was the routine every night when I was a kid. AM 1500: WJBK's Tom Clay. AM 1270: WXYZ's Lee Alan. AM 800: CKLW's Dave Shafer. All my idols. The Diamonds: "Little Darlin'." The Everly Brothers: "All I Have to Do Is Dream." Elvis Presley: "Love Me Tender." Some of the greatest music ever recorded. Sitting at my desk upstairs almost every night, doing homework, with the radio on loud enough to piss off the neighbors. I was in heaven!

Trouble was, I had to constantly turn the dial from one station to the next as the songs changed. But AM radio was of such poor quality that landing precisely on a new station required a fair amount of effort. Why don't tabletop radios have push buttons like the radios in most cars? Then again, some of you who have always had handheld stereo remote controls may not appreciate that that once was a problem.

I hitchhiked to a junkyard outside town; found a beautiful old Packard radio with an enclosed speaker right up front; hitchhiked to a TV repair shop uptown; asked how to make the radio work off regular 120-volt AC household plug-in power, not 12-volt DC car battery power; and assembled the parts just like the guy at the TV repair shop said; and it worked the first time I tried it.

Fantastic, no one had anything like it.

That's why I did things my way.

I knew I was never going to change that.

The thing that gave me my greatest pleasure; the thing that I came to realize I could do better than almost everyone else; the thing that became my greatest passion: doing things differently... original thinking...creativity...inventing.

Always questioning, always visualizing, always combining ideas from within my memory bank, always simplifying, always rationalizing. Repeat, repeat, repeat; over and over and over again. Endlessly starting again and again and again. A mind exercise that was always an adrenaline rush. Constant and tireless repetition. Forward steps, backward steps, countless repetition. Hours, days, months, and sometimes many years of struggle, all because of a vision, or perhaps only a yearning, to find a better way.

Occasionally a breakthrough. Sometimes a giant leap forward. Often a failure to reach full maturity, if for no other reason than the sheer scope of the endeavor. But one thing was always sure: there was never a time that my mind was idle or bored. I could always switch on one of the endless thoughts that were right there in the active area of my mind.

In fact, it was almost impossible ever to switch them off.

My life in a nutshell.

With a mechanical aptitude acquired through sheer necessity, a hands-on education that came from the technical high school I attended, and the engineering education I got in college, I was reasonably well equipped to undertake many of the technical challenges that I faced. That's not to say that I didn't wrestle with most of the other intellectual issues that I faced, but it was the technical side of life that I always found most rewarding. I had a knack for it: I could see things no one else could see.

The rudimentary, hands-on projects that I dealt with as a kid evolved to highly technical adult challenges that required the vision and inspiration that few others possessed. It was my strongest suit; it was the thing that I did best; and it was the thing that I enjoyed most.

The Overload Control Valve was a product that resulted from the university thesis work that I had done at Eaton Corporation's Engineering and Research Center. Industrial forklift trucks, one of Eaton Corporation's major products, occasionally tipped over while lifting or maneuvering heavy loads in warehouses and on loading docks. There was no way of telling whether the load was too heavy, or if the load was being extended too far out from the lift truck while it was being handled.

The Overload Control Valve was designed to detect the differential pressure in the lift truck's "tilt cylinders," which was proportional to the tipping tendency of the vehicle, and then to quickly and smoothly stop further elevation and/or forward extension of the load when the vehicle was at its overload threshold. On numerous occasions the system had to be demonstrated to Eaton's customers in a real warehouse environment: lift a near-capacity load of about five thousand pounds to a height of about forty feet, and then extend the load forward in the elevated position. The "pucker factor" was enormous: that damn Overload Control Valve had better stop the forward extension before the truck overturned, or we'd have one hell of a bad situation!

During the gasoline shortage and first oil embargo of the 1970s, the fuel economy of cars and trucks became important. The trouble was that there was no way of knowing exactly how a vehicle's fuel economy changed as driving conditions changed. Just how much better fuel economy did a car get at fifty-five miles per hour than it got at seventy miles per hour? And just how much was that jack-rabbit start costing in excess fuel consumption, anyway?

The technical solution to the real-time measurement of a vehicle's instantaneous fuel consumption, or miles per gallon, required precise measurement of fuel flow rate to the engine, with a compact, reliable, accurate, and low-cost device. Many attempts had been made, but no one had found the answer.

The heart of the problem was that fuel flow rate to an engine is minimal, even under relatively high demand circumstances. Nothing like water shooting from a garden hose; more like a pinhole leak in a milk container. Many attempts had been made to use impingement mechanisms, something like a pinwheel device that rotates as fuel flows past it, but those approaches were grossly inaccurate due to the minimal flow rate of the fuel.

Highly accurate, positive displacement devices, like rotating piston mechanisms, were in common use in instruments at the time, but they were prohibitively complex and expensive.

It was obvious that a low-cost, positive displacement device was the best answer, if it could be found. The solution was to utilize a small, precise cavity, about three times the size of a thimble, that could be filled with fluid and then emptied in a repetitive and continuous manner. Measuring the time interval that it took to fill the cavity would yield the precise flow rate of the fuel that was passing through the device and into the engine, and counting the number of times the cavity was filled would yield total fuel consumption.

A small sliding piston that moved back and forth in an enclosed cylindrical cavity made electrical contact at each end of its confined travel and fed into a computing circuit that measured the time interval between contacts. With this information, and with information that came from another device that measured the rotation frequency of the speedometer cable, it was possible to compute instantaneously the vehicle's miles per gallon, average miles per gallon, total fuel consumption, speed, and distance traveled. The Autocomputer had arrived.

The device was extraordinarily precise, very low cost, reliable, and compact. Management of the fuel vapors that were created in certain high-temperature environments turned out to be a problem that would have required relocation of the device closer to the vehicle's fuel tank and away from the heat of the engine compartment, but that final step was never completed before the project was made redundant by the universal conversion from carburetion systems to fuel injection that took place in the 1980s.

One of the most memorable flashes of insight that I've ever had came during the development process of the Autcomputer. I had been struggling for months with the problem that dirt and grime that was in all fuel systems could cause the sliding piston to stick after extensive use. I had never experienced the problem during testing, but I was worried about it nonetheless. Then one night, about three hours after I had retired to bed, I suddenly saw the answer in my mind. Not sure if it was a dream or just thoughts connected with another fitful night of trying unsuccessfully to turn the brain off. I jumped out of bed and searched for pencil and paper. In the middle of the night I sketched out a system that replaced the sliding piston with a brass accordion-type bellows that made no sliding contact as it moved between its electrical start and stop contact points. Worked great. Problem solved.

The best solutions to technical problems are usually the simplest. After they are discovered, it is often difficult to understand why they remained hidden for so long. How was it possible that someone hadn't stumbled across that particular idea long before then?

As is almost always the case, the answer is that we seem to be naturally programmed to see things as they already are. When we search for fresh ideas, our thinking tends to channel itself in a familiar direction. We know that that way works, and we're comfortable going there. A radically different approach is worrisome and threatening, so our subconscious mind seems to actively block the creative thought process. Original thinking must be learned through a lifetime spent questioning everything around us. It's a process that is gradually acquired, if it is acquired at all. When I think back on my life, I believe that I have worked with only three other individuals whom I would categorize as having truly exceptional creative talent.

One person with exceptional creative talent can make a greater contribution to technical advancement than thousands of others who do not have the ability. Leave the textbook solutions, the analysis methods, and the computer manipulations to those thousands. Leave the original thinking to the tiny minority who have spent a lifetime asking *why*, not *how*.

On the rare occasion when a person has real vision, the creative process can instantly shift to an extraordinarily high level. Two creative thinkers can lift each other simultaneously. Such was the case when a truly brilliant engineer at Bristol Compressors, Joe H, approached me with a preliminary idea on how to deactivate one of two cylinders in the air-conditioning compressors that we then annually produced by the millions. By deactivating one cylinder whenever full system capacity was not required, which was the majority of the time, system efficiency could be dramatically increased. From that original idea, we were able to leapfrog to a stunningly simple breakthrough idea that was soon to become the TS compressor.

When the light suddenly turned on in our minds, I, and I'm sure Joe as well, got a euphoric rush that happens on such rare occasions that it imprints itself in the mind, never to be forgotten. We had made a tremendous technical breakthrough that was applicable to the entire compressor line, yet was simultaneously simple and cost effective.

That kind of thing doesn't happen often. More often, an idea germinates in the mind over an extended period of time. Slowly and steadily it grows, evolving until it reaches the point when it can be converted to a rudimentary form of hardware. From there the creative process repeats itself over and over again as new and better ideas are incorporated. Sometimes the process can take years or even decades. Slowly inching along, taking two steps forward and one back, tracing and retracing the endless collection of ideas that must all come together successfully to make the whole.

The Golftote was one such idea. From the first time I played golf in the early 1980s, I wondered why it was necessary to carry around a full set of clubs when someone was simply trying to walk a quick round of golf after work. Thirteen clubs or more was too much to haul around a golf course in a bulky, heavy bag, even with a pushcart to lighten the load. No one was then playing for the country club championship; all they were trying to do was get some exercise and have a little fun doing it. Seemed like seven clubs, twelve balls, tees, a ball mark, and a green repair tool could all be conveniently carried in a device that stood upright in the ground with the aid of pins that stuck into the ground.

I had developed generation after generation of hardware over thirty years. The end product was a truly great creation, which unfortunately was never successfully commercially marketed. Had

I made more effort, and certain health issues not arisen, the idea might well have been highly successful in the marketplace.

A lifetime spent pursuing a seemingly endless number of new and different ideas: far more than can be mentioned in this writing. Twenty-three patents and file drawers full of ideas.

The effort continues as vigorously as ever. Wonder which ideas I'll be wrestling with when the end finally comes?

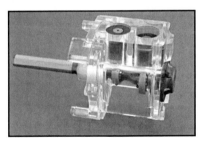
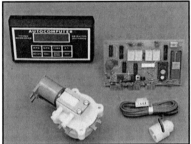

Chapter 19
Common Sense

I must have rewritten this chapter a half dozen times or more, and every time I reread what I wrote I realized that I had missed the point almost entirely. So maybe what you'll read here won't be much better than the versions you will never see…but I hope that's not the case.

In writing this account of my life, my primary objective was to avoid generating a monotonous recitation of events. It was more important to me that I convey only the most meaningful and emotional experiences that were part of my life. I hoped that if I could accomplish that objective I would reveal who I was and what really mattered to me in an indirect but clear and concise manner. I had such a difficult time writing this chapter because what follows deviates from that objective.

The following is a simple recitation (there's that word I've been trying to avoid) of several fundamental principles that have always guided me. If there is a redeeming quality to what is written here, it is that I always had a strong emotional attachment to these principles. These have been the most important directional markers, the things that have strongly motivated me.

Question everything

I never accepted things as they were; I always tried to find a better way of doing things. Finding those new and better methods was my principal goal. So I never asked the question: Is there a better way? There always was. The question that I did ask was: Does what I see warrant the effort that would be required for me to change it? It is true that most things I encountered never justified my full attention or presented me with an opportunity to affect them. Obviously, there was not enough time to deal with everything. But things did fall into the category that necessitated my intervention. When I encountered them, I always sought to find a better way.

To do that, I was never hesitant to throw out the rule book, or at a minimum, rewrite the rules. That was scary for most people because they lived by the rules, and when those rules were taken away they often got lost. That was never the case for me. It was obvious that progress only came when things changed, so I always tried to get out of the rut of tradition and to venture into uncharted waters. My life would have been stagnant and uneventful if I hadn't constantly searched for better ways of doing things.

I was always well aware that failure frequently is the result of change. It happened often, and when it did I found it was necessary to try again and again and again. Eventual success usually produced benefits that far outweighed the cost of the setbacks.

When I ran different businesses I always preached that we had to question everything we did and then constantly search for a better way of doing things. I wanted everyone in the company to try again and again to improve processes. I repeatedly assured them that failure in the pursuit of change was common, expected, and acceptable. If at the end of the year you had told me that you succeeded every time you tried something new, I would have told you that you hadn't pushed hard enough to change things; when you pursue change, you often fail!

Build a strong foundation

The Egyptians eventually figured it out, and building codes everywhere now spell it out in great detail: how to build a strong foundation. If that pyramid you're building is to last for thousands of years, and if that bridge across the river is to remain standing, they had better be built on strong foundations. Almost everyone seemed to understand the idea as it pertained to construction projects, but so many never seemed to realize that building a strong foundation was equally important in their personal lives. Why was that?

I realized early on in my life that there were no shortcuts to success. If I wanted the good things in life, I had to prepare myself before those things would come my way. There were no simple ways to build life's foundation. Everything required hard work, attention to detail, and the seemingly endless denial of short-term rewards. Just like every brick, board, and nail that goes into a home's foundation must be put in place one at a time, so too are the life skills that have to be learned.

The same principles applied to building a successful business. Each department, each operation, each functional part of the business had to be examined in detail and changed as necessary to enable it to excel. There were no shortcuts as some would have you believe. How many times had I heard: "All we really need to do is…"

Keep it simple

I'd seen it countless times before: business managers who were lost in a world that they didn't understand, never realizing that successful management required nothing more than common sense. It mattered not the type of business, its size, its complexity, or where it was located. Basic management principles were always the same: the application of the commonsense things that everyone should have learned through everyday experiences.

That's not to say that the skills required to master the numerous disciplines in a company were easy to come by. Not at all. If you want to be an engineer, you have to develop your engineering skills; to work in manufacturing, you have to understand complex machinery; for finance, you need to study accounting. But to manage, all that is really required is a clear mind and an understanding of numerous basic principles.

It didn't take a genius to understand it, and it wasn't difficult to do, but it was often hard to find. Even when the method was repeatedly demonstrated, there were frequently blank faces on those who were certain that management required obfuscation in the work place: Applied Information Economics, Capability

Maturity Model Integration, Earned Value Management, Functional Economic Analysis, Matrix Management, Six Sigma…

That was the kind of stuff you might hear from MBAs who believed themselves to be on management's leading edge. The world was full of them; in fact, that mind-set was more often the rule than the exception. What a shame it was that so many corporate leaders didn't know how to lead a company. They weren't even in the game; they were clueless.

If I had ever started a business management school, the first, the last, and the only course I would have taught would have been called *Common Sense*. Back to basics, keep it simple, common sense: it really wasn't complicated.

Appreciate

The approach in both my personal life and my business endeavors was always the same: treat everyone with respect, dignity, courtesy, honesty, fairness, and consideration. Those were the indicators that showed appreciation for the other person. There was nothing complicated about it, but it sure was effective. Time after time, it kept them coming back for more. Why wouldn't they? Those were the basic needs that everyone had. Recipients invariably responded in a positive manner, which often resulted in successful communications and interactions.

That's how I dealt with Mrs. Green when I cut her grass: *Yeah, Betty, I would highly recommend that kid if you want your grass cut; he's so polite.*

That's how I dealt with that middle-aged couple who were looking for a camera: *Let's find that guy who was so helpful last fall when we couldn't figure out how to use our old camera; I'm sure he'll give us good advice on the new camera we're looking for.*

That's how I interacted with the janitor who emptied my trash and swept my office floor when I was a junior engineer: *I like the way he treats me; not like some of those other guys who don't even know that I exist.*

That's how I related to the supervisor out on the production floor: *You know I really hope he gets that vice president position; he always seems to have a straightforward, positive approach to solving problems.*

What it all comes down to is that you really have to give a damn about everyone else…that you have to realize that others are every bit as important as you are…that they have families who depend on them…that they laugh, cry, worry, and grieve just like you do. So if you are going to deal with them, you need to think first about how *you* want to be treated. Then stand back and open your eyes; everything is right there in front of you.

But it was really funny; you couldn't teach others how to do it. They had to have learned it for themselves along the way. And you could tell if they had almost as soon as they opened their mouth.

Chapter 20
Beautiful Brown-Eyed Girl

Those big, beautiful brown eyes, that gorgeous auburn hair, and a body shaped to perfection; those were the things that you noticed first. When she looked at you and smiled just a little, you knew that this one was really special. There was something very mysterious and very sexual about her that couldn't easily be put into words. What was it about the way she talked and the way she moved that was so magnetic? She was different from all the others; you just had to get to know her.

And the closer we got, the more interesting she became. But you knew that there was still so much to learn, and so much more that you could never learn. And it wasn't long before you realized that you couldn't live without her. And it wasn't long after that you realized you couldn't live with her. So that morning when we were lying in bed together, each sharing secrets that had always been kept hidden deep inside, I was completely speechless when she said, "I want to marry you."

I wasn't surprised; our relationship had already developed into a fantastic affair unlike any that I had ever known, even though it seemed like I'd been through at least a million relationships before. So I knew it was coming; and it felt so good to know that she felt that way. But oh god, what do I say now? There was no worse place to be: knowing that I couldn't live without her and at the same time realizing that I couldn't live with her, either.

Intelligent, well educated, good-natured, and down to earth with an air of sophistication; that's who she was. In my eyes no one was more attractive, better dressed, or more graceful. And her mysterious and sexual nature was extremely compelling. So it was no surprise that she was constantly on my mind. Not just when we were together, but always. Driving alone in my car she was there with me. Walking down the aisle of a grocery store, I would look at an item on the shelf and subconsciously ask myself if she would like it.

I was truly in love. Not for the first time in my life, but in a way I had not known before.

But watch out, my friend. When suspicion and distrust charge into the middle of a relationship, all hope can eventually be lost. You can try to manage it, reason with it, plead with it, and shout it down, but sooner or later it must come to its senses or disaster will follow. And when those thoughts are in someone else's head, not your own, those issues are particularly difficult to deal with. Why can't you see that I'm not at all interested in her, or her, or her? It's you that I love; why can't you understand that?

Why is my security system's alarm going off in the middle of the day like this? Oh, hi, I didn't know you were coming over. I came home from work to get some sleep; couldn't keep my eyes open. Just getting back from my Asian trip yesterday, I guess that's to be expected...What are you talking about? I was sound asleep when you came in and set off the alarm...Because I just got back from Asia yesterday and I was dead tired...What? There's no one else here; I was sleeping. There's no one in the house except you and me, you can see that, can't you? Then go ahead and look around and see for yourself.

Why can't you understand that I wasn't with someone else? We've been arguing about this for two solid hours. You've never seen me do anything that could remotely be construed in that way. Not before, not now, not ever. I can't keep going on like this... You've got to go now. I want you to leave. I think we need to put off the wedding. Marriage won't work if you're constantly thinking this way.

It just keeps getting worse and worse. Here we are walking down Fifth Avenue, nice-looking women everywhere; in fact, the sidewalks are so crowded that we can hardly get by. No, I wasn't fantasizing about her, or her, or her. They're right there in front of us; how can I not see them? Yes, that bigger-than-life picture of the model in the window of that clothing boutique is really something, but no, I'm not fantasizing about her either. Why are you constantly bringing that stuff up? You know you've got me so self-conscious that I find that I don't even turn my head anymore when we walk down the street.

We've been together for four years now, and they've been the best years of my life in almost every way, but you've got to get over this stuff. I could understand it if I was coming home at three in the morning, smelling of perfume, with blond hairs on my jacket. But that hasn't happened. Nothing suspicious has happened and you know that. Are you thinking like this because your ex constantly hid his drug problem from you until that house of cards came tumbling down? Is it because your work as a therapist exposes you to that hidden world that few others ever see? Is it because you yourself have been involved with other guys who led that life? Is that a life you've led? What is it?

No, not my assistant. Not our chief legal officer. Not either one of my ex's. Not my California friend. Not that person I was talking to on the phone the other day. You can see every part of my life from the inside. You're at my home when I'm traveling. Ever seen a piece of mail, heard a voice mail, read an e-mail, or seen someone show up at the door who seemed suspicious?

We weren't whispering to each other at the party. The only thing that you didn't know about was the cake that she got to celebrate your birthday. I'm not seeing her on the side. Where do you come up with these things?

You know I didn't know it at the time, but those red marks on my stomach and legs weren't bug bites, they were poison oak. I've had it several times since we parted. Wish I would have realized it at the time so that I might have convinced you that I wasn't out somewhere on my property screwing someone else. Too bad you had to make such a big thing out of it. We had had such a great evening together up until that point. Lying there on the bed and scratching like that sure did get your mind going, didn't it? Okay, that's it. I can't do this anymore. You're the love of my life. I'll never get over you. But I've got to say good-bye.

This hurts so much; I know I'll never get over it. Never. But now I've got to figure out how to survive just one more day, one more hour, maybe just one more minute. I knew it would be like this; there was never any doubt in my mind. Why in the hell do I have so many pictures of her throughout my home? Can't turn anywhere without seeing her. Just picking them all up and putting them in that box is extraordinarily painful. Maybe it's a good thing that red eyes are a little bit difficult to see through.

The only reason I'd stayed in Pennsylvania after retiring was because of her, but I couldn't stay there any longer. If I had any chance of survival, I had to get out of Pennsylvania immediately.

Yes, that's the price for the home and all the furnishings but only if we can close in less than seven days. Didn't know that a deal could be done so fast. Here are the keys; enjoy your new home. Got to make this drive back to Kansas nonstop, except for gas.

I'm hurting so bad, Harvey, I just don't know what to do. She is too? She said that? Of course I'll talk to her if she calls. Hi. Yes, I'm hurting that bad too. That would be great. Fly into Wichita as soon as you can. We'll see if we can work things out.

Hi, beautiful girl; you'll never know how much I've missed you.

Those pictures we took of that spectacular California sunset over the water in Monterey were the saddest pictures I've ever seen. Never have been able to look at them again. There we were together, for the last time. Prophetic, wasn't it, the sun setting behind us like that? The sun that had risen again with all the hope that comes with a new day was to set again, but far too quickly.

No, beautiful girl, I can hardly remember anything about that night in California after we had that last terrible breakup. You know I took that sleeping aid so that I could make it all go away and when I awoke you were gone. I remember you crying so hard as I was falling asleep, but I didn't hear you leave. I've always regretted that I really never said a final good-bye. Did you say good-bye to me while I was sleeping? Yes, I got your note, and I found the engagement ring there on the desk.

So let me now say good-bye, beautiful brown-eyed girl. I'll always love you, and I'll never get over you.

And I've never gotten over you.

So here's a Ronnie Milsap song that's just for you:

I Wouldn't Have Missed It for the World

Our paths may never cross again
Maybe my heart will never mend
But I'm glad for all the good times
Cause you've brought me so much sunshine
And love was the best it's ever been

I wouldn't have missed it for the world
Wouldn't have missed loving you girl
You've made my whole life worth while, with your smile

I wouldn't trade one memory
Cause you mean too much to me
Even though I lost you girl
I wouldn't have missed it for the world

They say that all good things must end
Love comes and goes just like the wind
You've got your dreams to follow
But if I had the chance tomorrow
You know I'd do it all again

I wouldn't have missed it for the world
Wouldn't have missed loving you girl
You've made my whole life worth while, with your smile

I wouldn't trade one memory
Cause you mean too much to me
Even though I lost you girl
I wouldn't have missed it for the world

Oh I wouldn't trade one memory
Cause you mean too much to me
Even though I lost you girl
I wouldn't have missed it for the world

I wouldn't have missed it for the world
Wouldn't have missed loving you girl
You've made my whole life worth while
With your smile

Chapter 21
Traveling On

Several of my cousins from my mother's side of the family were quite a bit older than me, so I naturally looked up to them with a certain degree of admiration. They were the pioneers, the adventurers, the ones who seemed to lead the way. After finishing high school, some of them packed their bags and headed west to seek their fortunes. How I envied them; they seemed to have a vision that was soon to become my vision: to see the world.

I hadn't yet reached my teenage years but I knew even then that I wanted to see as much of the world as possible. I had no idea how I was going to do that, but if some of my cousins could get as far away as California, that dreamland I had heard so much about, then I could do it too. But how? I hadn't yet been far from my home state of Michigan. All I could really brag about was traveling to a foreign country, Canada, which was just across the Detroit River, about thirty miles from my doorstep. That hardly seemed to count at all. No, I hadn't seen anything that really mattered. Not yet, anyway.

When I was fifteen, one of my friends, who was also fifteen, got a pilot's license and asked if I wanted to fly around the local area in his Piper Cub. I hadn't been on an airplane before, so I jumped at the opportunity. Somehow or another he managed to get that old piece of junk up in the air and then down again without killing us both. The first time we hit a downdraft it kind of freaked me out, but I didn't express alarm. Mission accomplished, but I still hadn't gone anywhere that really mattered yet.

It wasn't long after that my traveling adventures took a definite turn for the better. Dad decided that he, my brother, and I should take a driving trip through the southern and eastern United States. Mom didn't come because Dad tended to drive in a manner that scared her half to death. In any case, I was about to take my first baby steps in my quest to see the world.

It was funny how my preconceived notions about the areas we visited all proved to be true. They talked funny in Louisiana, which tended to make everyone with whom we came in contact seem strange. And those New York City folks were awfully rude and aloof. I could hardly imagine what people would be like in a different country, but I was anxious to find out.

Since my family didn't have the money to spend on frivolous adventures, I had to live vicariously through the few friends I had who were able to travel abroad. When my friend Roy and his wife came back from England, France, and Germany, I inundated them with questions: how, what, where, who…

Soon after I started working at Eaton Corporation's Engineering and Research Center, I got a lucky break that helped greatly in my mission to see all of the United States. Eaton was a member of the Western Highway Institute, a trucking organization that was located in California. A meeting of that organization was scheduled to be held in Chicago, in the middle of winter. Several of the more senior engineers had turned down the opportunity to attend the meeting as representatives of Eaton, so when I was asked, I jumped at the opportunity. Chicago in January? I can deal with that.

Then an interesting thing happened. At the last minute the meeting was rescheduled for the next fall in San Francisco, so my chance to see the land of my dreams would come at last. In preparation for the trip I decided to include a stopover in Denver. This was a practice that I adopted for virtually all of the business travel that I would do in the future: always stop to visit some other place that I had not yet seen that was in the general vicinity of my destination. I always paid the extra cost of the diversion out of my own pocket, and I always used my vacation time. By so doing I was able to see far more of the world than I otherwise would have seen. My continuing involvement in the Western Highway Institute enabled me to see most of the western United States because meeting venues were constantly changing.

My time at Eaton also required travel to many other parts of the United States.

Once I was flying into Philadelphia with another engineer. Just as the plane touched down on the runway, my fellow engineer, who was looking out the window as we landed, exclaimed in an elevated and panicked voice that something was wrong with the wing. I, and everyone around us, suddenly turned to the nearest window to try to figure out what the problem was. Was the wing failing as we raced down the runway at over one hundred miles per hour? No, nothing quite as dramatic as that. The pilot had simply raised the wing flaps and activated the reverse thrusters as pilots always do when they land. How embarrassing. For a split second I wondered if a wing failure might have been a better outcome.

On another trip a few months later, we were about to depart the same airport in Philadelphia. The pilot pushed the throttle forward and we began to race down the runway. Faster and faster, farther and farther down the runway we went…should be lifting off any time now. Faster and faster, farther and farther. Wonder when we're going to lift off? Then suddenly the pilot slammed on the brakes, reversed the thrusters, and came to a stop at the very end of the runway. Silence. What the hell just happened? Then the pilot came on the PA system and said, "I think we'll try that one again, folks." Nothing more, nothing less. Ahhhh…how in the hell do I get off this plane?

Trying to get off an airplane at 36,000 feet is a really bad idea, but it almost seemed like a reasonable option during one of my numerous transcontinental flights. Back in those days, meals were served to all passengers on relatively long flights. First down the aisle on that dreadful day was the drink cart, but the meal service cart was still a long way up the aisle. "Would you like something to drink, sir?" Yes, I'll have a tomato juice, please. Don't need it in a glass; I can leave it in the can on this fold-out table until my meal arrives.

Sure took a long time for the meal to arrive, but it finally showed up. The tomato juice had been sitting there for a long time so I decided to shake it up vigorously. Shake, shake, shake, shake…oh no, no, no…the flight attendant had already opened the can, but I didn't realize that. Tomato juice flew everywhere. Somewhere around a dozen passengers had gotten soaked to one extent or another. Seemed like *they* were going to open a door at 36,000 feet and throw me out. Wasn't sure if that was such a bad alternative at the time.

That was just the tip of the iceberg. The nearly constant world travel that was required by the international companies that I worked for throughout my career gave me the chance to see every state in the union and many countries in every region of the world.

My first international trip didn't happen until I started working for Rockwell International in the late 1970s. That trip took me to England, Germany, Austria, France, Switzerland, and Italy. The business portion of that trip was limited to Germany and Italy; the other countries came on my own time and at my own expense. To get everything possible from the trip I drove from Munich to Milan, stopping along the way to take in as much of the area as possible. Lasting impressions included London's similarity to New York City, Munich's order and cleanliness, the beauty of the resort town of Baden-Baden, the pink hotel in Karlsruhe, the cosmopolitan nature of Zurich, the spectacular scenic beauty of the Alps, and the chaotic nature of Milan and Torino.

To this day I can still see the exceptionally well ordered manufacturing plants in Germany. All the machines were freshly painted, the floors were spotless, and the workforce wore matching uniforms. The thing that impressed me most was the attention to detail that was evident everywhere I looked. Every desk was impeccably organized: papers were in neat stacks that were perfectly squared with the desktop; pens and pencils were grouped and in perfect vertical alignment with the sides of the desk. When I noticed that all of the empty soft drink bottles were perfectly aligned in their containers next to the vending machine, I realized that order was an obsession with these people. I liked what I saw and immediately adopted similar practices in my own life. My kids still laugh when they see me repositioning things around the house.

But Germany had a dark side to its past: the Dachau concentration camp, one of the most infamous sites in Germany, was located only about ten miles from the beautiful city of Munich. Visiting the site left a lasting impression on me that has not diminished in any way, even after all the years that have passed.

One image that was vividly imprinted in my mind was a large photograph of bodies stacked in the center of one of the rooms in the camp. At the edge of the photograph, a large window, which was hinged on its edge, was swung open and certain other features of the room could be identified. As I was standing at the entrance to the room in which the photograph was displayed, I saw an open window that was identical to the one in the photograph. It suddenly became apparent that the photograph must have been taken from the very spot at which I was standing. Bam! It hit me right between the eyes. It all became so real.

It's difficult to fathom that the more than forty-one thousand people who died at the camp was a small number compared to how many died in the Auschwitz/Birkenau and Treblinka extermination camps.

In the years that have followed I have revisited Dachau several times and have also seen the Auschwitz/Birkenau and Treblinka extermination camps, the Babi Yar and Rumbula massacre sites, and the ghettos in Budapest, Krakow, Minsk, Prague, Riga, Vienna, and Vilnius. I have searched for some understanding of how something like that could have happened, but I find no answers.

Most of my travel during my time at Rockwell was to Western Europe. By the time I left to join Bristol Compressors, I had seen virtually every country in that region, but my travels had yet to take me to Central or Eastern Europe, Asia, the Middle East, the Far East, Asia Pacific, or South America.

Bristol Compressors was another story. As the CEO of an international company, I traveled regularly to see customers, suppliers, agents, and political persons around the world. Much of that travel was to parts of the world that most travelers seldom see. For example, Bristol did a lot of business in the Middle East, the Far East, and South America.

When I first traveled to Saudi Arabia, I stood in line at immigration for about four hours for some ridiculous reason or another. But it was all worth the effort, if for no other reason than to see how fabulous oil wealth can affect a country. During subsequent trips to the region I was able to see Egypt, Israel, Kuwait, all of the United Arab Emirates, Dubai, Qatar, Bahrain, and Oman.

During one trip to Saudi Arabia I was shown a huge housing complex that was probably greater than a square mile in area. There were towering block walls around the perimeter of the site with several monitored gates for entrance and departure. Intermixed with the apartment-style housing units were all the retail establishments that were required to make the development self-sustaining. My associates explained to me that the development had been built to provide housing for the countless expatriates from all over the world who were living and working in Saudi. Apparently the Saudi government had second thoughts about congregating such a large number of foreign workers in one place. The possibility of civil unrest concerned them to such an extent that they decided not to occupy the complex, so there it stood totally empty, an embarrassment to the government.

It was for that reason the government prohibited anyone from taking pictures of the site or from lingering in the area. Of course I didn't feel that the prohibition applied to me, so I asked our driver to stop at a vantage point on a hill overlooking the area so I could take a picture. No way, I was repeatedly told; there will be real trouble if we do that.

Come on, come on, I said, look around, there's no one here to see us. I want a picture of this. My persistence paid off, much to the chagrin of those who were with me.

By the time I had clicked the camera shutter the third time, we were surrounded by Saudi police. As translated by my associates, I came to understand that we were being arrested and were to be taken to a police station in the area. It didn't look good; not at all.

After perhaps two hours of pleading, my associates were able to get us out of the jam we were in. The only thing we had going for us was that the business my associates worked for was owned by one of the sons of the king of Saudi Arabia. After numerous communications over the police radio, it was finally established that we were well connected enough through the government that we should be released with nothing worse than me having my camera confiscated. Sometimes you just get lucky.

Sometimes lucky, sometimes unlucky.

One evening, while I was staying in a hotel in Riyadh, Saudi Arabia, I went for a long walk with a business associate who represented us in various regions of the world. He had a busy European travel schedule ahead of him, and he wasn't sure how he was going to be able to make the numerous connections that he had to make all over Europe; the commercial flights that were available to him couldn't be made to work.

No problem, I said. Why don't you charter a plane to take you where you need to go? I had done that myself on occasion, and it sure made things easier. Of course it was costly, but sometimes you need to do what you need to do. No, he said, he never used chartered planes because they didn't have great safety records. Get over it, I said; you need to make it work for you. Stop worrying.

About two weeks later my executive assistant came into my office with bad news. Our representative, the man who had expressed concern over flying on a chartered plane, had been killed when his chartered plane had flown into a storm while crossing the Alps.

Don't let me talk you into anything: not a chartered flight, not a photograph...nothing!

Bristol's business in the Far East and South America allowed me to see Japan, South Korea, Taiwan, Hong Kong, China, Venezuela, Brazil, Argentina, and Chile. Plenty of stories there; some to be found elsewhere in this writing. Here are few more.

I was once flying from Beijing to Hong Kong on a Chinese domestic airline. In the mid-1980s China often flew old aircraft that had seen extended service with other airlines around the world. I boarded the plane, looked around, and began to wonder what I had gotten myself into. An old, decrepit, filthy, smelly, jam-packed plane. Had the pilots ridden bikes to the airport? But off we went, not realizing that the best was yet to come.

Anyone who has ever flown into the old Kai Tak Airport in Hong Kong can relate to this story. To approach the airport, pilots had to fly low over the city, not much higher than many of the city's buildings. That is one of the reasons the airport was known as one of the five most difficult airports in the world to fly into. During the approach you could literally look out the window at people hanging their laundry out to dry on their apartment balconies. A challenging landing for even the best pilots in good weather conditions.

The plane I was on was trying to land in bad weather. Driving rain and wind were making it difficult to line up the plane with the runway; that was obvious to anyone looking out the window. As we approached touchdown, I saw only grass, no runway. Then full thrusters were summoned and we headed skyward again; an aborted landing. Off we went to circle the airport and try again. The second attempt was no different from the first: driving rain and wind made it difficult to stay lined up with the runway. What runway? All I see is grass. Nose up, full thrusters; around we went again.

Zero for two on our attempted landings. Driving rain, buildings to the right of us, buildings to the left of us. An old, decrepit, filthy, smelly, jam-packed plane. Had the pilots ridden bikes to the airport? Not a confidence builder.

We finally landed without incident.

That experience was bad enough, but there's another airplane story that goes way beyond it as measured on the "scare the crap out of you" index.

The year was somewhere around 1986. Bristol Compressors had scheduled a board of directors meeting for a Friday in Washington, DC. I was on a flight from Charlotte, North Carolina, to Washington National Airport. As we were approaching the airport from the south, our pilot came on the PA system to tell us that a thunderstorm was approaching the airport from the north and we were going to have to fly into the leading edge of the storm, then turn around and fly out of the storm to land. He warned us that there would be severe turbulence, but once we flew back out of the leading edge of the storm things would calm down as we landed. Oh well, I thought, that's what these guys get paid to do. They're experts at this kind of thing; not to worry.

As we approached the leading edge of the storm, all hell broke loose. I had never experienced anything like it before, nor have I experienced anything like it since. I was amazed that the plane stayed in one piece. As we approached the airport, conditions hardly improved at all. The approach path to Washington National Airport is fairly difficult even in good weather because planes must avoid flying near numerous government buildings for security reasons. Extreme weather made the job far more difficult. Just as we were about to touch down, the pilot applied full engine thrust and up we went again into a very stormy sky.

Okay, okay, I thought to myself. It was clear that trying to land in that kind of weather had been a mistake, but we had gotten away with it. Now we would have to find an alternative landing site. It had been a bad decision by the pilots, but at least we had gotten away with it. Live and learn. They wouldn't soon do anything like that again.

Or would they?

You guessed it. Around they went again to make another landing attempt. But by then the storm was centered near the airport. Our first attempted landing had been an extreme experience, but what we were now experiencing was even worse. What in the world those pilots were thinking was beyond my understanding. Perhaps alternate airports weren't any better than Washington National. Perhaps we didn't have enough fuel to go anywhere else. Perhaps our pilots were idiots. I'll never know the answer. I did know that the second landing attempt that we were about to make could have serious consequences.

We were all over the sky, and the plane was falling and rising in the extreme. Then, as we were attempting to make a sharp turn, the plane suddenly seemed to fall from the sky and nearly roll over. A hard bank in the opposite direction created a severe roll in the other direction. Fortunately, we had enough altitude to regain some semblance of control. We landed fast, somewhat sideways, and very long on the runway. The screaming passengers eventually settled down and everyone walked away with the realization that a disastrous ending had somehow been avoided.

Here's the funny part of the story. After spending the weekend following the board meeting in Washington, DC, I was getting dressed in my hotel room on Monday morning while I watched one of the network morning shows on television. One of the segments on the show dealt with wind shear problems that pilots sometimes face when they're trying to land in unsettled weather. There was a pressing need for wind shear detectors at major airports, the pilot who was being interviewed said. Then he began talking about the severe wind shear that he had experienced on the previous Friday

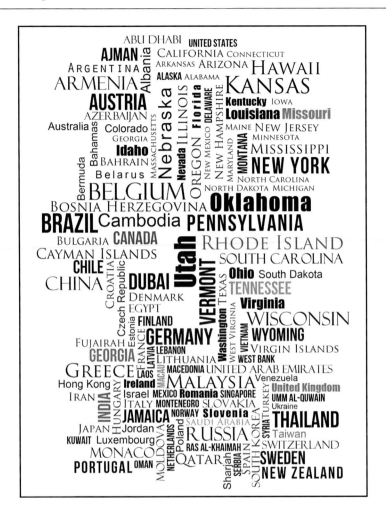

while attempting a landing at Washington National. The wind shear was so severe, he said, that it nearly led to a crash landing. He was talking about the flight that I had been on.

Harrowing experiences related to my time at Bristol Compressors didn't end with the Washington National flight. During the time I was away and running Evcon Industries, Bristol had entered into a joint venture with Carrier Corporation to build compressors in Agra, India. When I returned to Bristol for the second time, this misguided venture was just one more problem that I had to deal with firsthand, so off I went by car from Delhi to Agra. By Indian drivers' standards, the 150 miles could be covered in less than an hour, if you just drove fast enough. You would understand the comment if you've ever been on the roads in India.

I've seen my share of insane driving practices around the world, but in my opinion there is no place that is more chaotic than India. There are no rules; anything goes. Stoplights are ignored. Drive on either side of the road whenever you want. Pass on a hill or curve; no need to see oncoming traffic. It's one continuous game of chicken. Cutting someone off, or pulling right in front of someone, is standard practice. If your vehicle breaks down in the middle of the road, just stop right there and fix it.

So picture the car that I was in, heading from Delhi to Agra, at a high speed, weaving in and out of traffic, passing on hills and

curves, ignoring stoplights, cutting off everyone else on the road, and then suddenly, and without any warning, the front hood of the car unlatches and the hood flies up and completely covers the front windshield so that the driver is driving blind…at somewhere around eighty miles per hour.

There must be some reason, unknown to me at present, why I've been given so many additional chances.

Chapter 22
Big John Is Back

It was only about 120 miles east and south of Rome, but it still took quite a while to get there. Frosinone was as close as we were going to get by train, so we would have to do the last leg of the journey by taxi. Isola del Liri and Sora, see, they're right next to each other on this map. Can you take us there? Great!

Mom always said that her parents came from one of the most beautiful parts of Italy, but until you saw it for yourself you had no way of knowing. And since she had never seen Italy herself, you had to assume that all she really knew about the beauty of this far-away land she had learned from her mother. As the taxi weaved its way through the valley, the Liri River and the Apennine Mountains were breathtaking. Looks like this journey into the past is going to be even better than I had hoped, and far more emotional, too.

I love the way you do that, Ma, holding the tips of your fingers and thumb together as you gesture up and down with your hand while you're talking. I remember you and Grandma going back and forth like that whenever the two of you got into a heated conversation. Talk about emotion...but then that's the Italian way, isn't it? I know, I know, Ma, northern Italy, not from Sicily where those gangsters come from. You've made that perfectly clear many times before.

So tell me that story again, Ma. Your mother was the most beautiful girl in her village but her family was so poor that they didn't even have a mirror, so she had to look at her image in the river? Sounds a lot like a fairy-tale story, doesn't it? But if you say that's the way it was, then that's the way it was. I really like hearing those stories, so tell me more.

She was really young when she met Grandpa down by the river that day. A real good-looking guy from the neighboring town of Sora, which was just up river from Isola del Liri. Kind of swept her off her feet, I guess. Said he was going to marry her when he got back to Italy after going to America to find out what that new world was all about. She believed him and said that she would wait? Must have been a pretty convincing guy.

Grandma's father liked John, but her mother wasn't having any part of him. Night after night, Grandma said, she would lie in bed listening to her mother rant and rave to her father: "He's the devil, he's the devil. He's not marrying my daughter." But in his quiet voice her father continually reassured her that John would be good for their daughter.

Maybe Grandma's mother was bothered because Grandpa had

the reputation of being a tough guy. Once someone slashed him in the back of the neck with a razor while he was playing cards in a saloon. Guess he later tracked the guy down and settled the score. Who knows, but I'm guessing Grandma's mother figured it wasn't likely he'd come back from America, so she had nothing to worry about, anyway. But then again, if he did come back one day…

Sure enough, that day did come. As the story goes, someone from the village got advance notice that John was back from America. Word immediately went out: "Big John is back! Big John is back!" Everyone who came out into the streets must have seen quite a spectacle. There he was, striding confidently through the center of town with a handlebar mustache that must have been at least fourteen inches from tip to tip, and a large stash of polished gold coins inserted into his money belt. And all that he was heard to say was, "I've come back for Frances."

So the coins in his money belt were all polished? And he said he had come back for Frances? I wonder how those details weren't forgotten after all the years. Makes sense to me, though; that's entirely in keeping with the man himself. Strong and confident; undoubtedly worshipped by almost everyone in the village. That was my mother's father; that was my grandfather. Guess we must have come from some pretty good stock, right, Ma?

It's not hard to understand why your family was so poor, though, Ma. Trying to raise eight surviving kids in America on the ten dollars a day that Ford Motor Company was paying couldn't have been easy. Especially since your father couldn't read or write. I know Grandma used to read to him at night until she couldn't keep her eyes open any longer and wanted to stop. And I remember your telling me that he would say, "No, no, keep on reading. We're just getting to the good part." And so on and on she would read; you didn't argue with John, did you?

I guess that's worth repeating, eh, Ma? He ruled with an iron hand. It was going to be his way, period. Even your neighbors were afraid of him. And you kids did what you were told, didn't you? I've always loved the part about how he would never let you kids go out to have any fun, so you always had to tell him that you were going to the library. Guess those were the magic words. Mention education and he would agree to anything. Funny how being illiterate can affect you. You must have gone to the library some of those times, though, Ma, because you sure did learn a lot.

Look at that sign over there, Madelon, just off to the right

side of the road: Isola del Liri 30 kilometers/Sora 60 kilometers. We'll be there before you know it. This countryside is breathtaking; why would Grandma and Grandpa have left a place like this?

Isola del Liri. Wow, this town is much bigger and much nicer than I had expected. Where did I get the idea that this was a tiny outpost with nothing much going for it? Look how the river splits in two, goes around the town, and then reconnects at the far end of town. That's why they called it Isola del Liri; it really is an island on the Liri River.

Narrow streets, quaint shops, outdoor cafés, wrinkled old men and women busy doing nothing that seems all that important: this is my heritage. I can just picture Grandma walking around the corner and stopping to look up at this spectacular waterfall at the far edge of town. And that old castle at the top of the falls

has probably been watching over this town for hundreds of years. Must have looked down on Grandma, too, and her parents' parents' parents' parents' parents.

Can't imagine how many times Grandpa must have stood here too. You can't track down the most beautiful girl in town by staying home in Sora all the time, now can you?

The name Sora doesn't sound nearly as nice as Isola del Liri, does it? But the town itself has every bit as much appeal. Cobbled streets accented by colorful storefronts, trees, and flowers, all complement the Liri River, which runs through the center of town. Even the colorful laundry that's hung out to dry on lines strung between buildings adds to the beauty.

Hello, my name is Michael Young and this is my friend Madelon Marie. Sorry, neither one of us speaks Italian. The books all say that the municipal records office is the best place to begin a genealogical search, that's why we've come here. We're searching for my family's historical records. My grandfather's surname was Secondini or Secondino, I've seen it spelled both ways. His first name was Giovanni. He was born on March 28, 1872. His hometown was here in Sora. Can you help us find him in your records?

Ma, I sure wish I could have made this trip forty years ago. If I had, I could have told you so many things that I've discovered about your side of the family. I'll bet even your mother and father didn't know some of what I now know.

Since you never told me, I have to assume that you never knew that when your father's grandfather was a newborn infant he was left in the "wheel" at Santa Maria Assunta Church in Sora. Apparently it was common at that time for abandoned children to be left in a rotating wheel on an outside wall of a church. The wheel could be turned so that the infant would end up inside the church, where it would hopefully be found and cared for. In this way the person abandoning the child could remain anonymous.

The municipal records show that the infant found on January 3, 1810, was the second abandoned child to be found in Sora that year. With no known family name, it appears that he was given the surname Secondino, meaning second, because he was the second abandoned baby found that year. The name Secondino cannot be found in any records that predate that period. I wonder if there was a stigma attached to the Secondino name that Giuseppe had to live with?

Ma, it's difficult to put into words the excitement and the emotion that overcame me as we looked at the original documents that were kept at the records office and the library and churches in Sora that we subsequently visited. No computer records, no photocopies, just the original books with tattered pages. Handwritten entries that noted birth, marriage, death, and other significant dates of all family members were not copies; they were all original.

Want to know the name of the wet nurse who was paid to care for Giuseppe? The exact location of the family property? A family member's occupation? It's all there, Ma, and I'm going to organize it all so that my kids' kids' kids' kids' kids will know who we are and how in the hell we got here.

Yeah, Great-great-great-great-great-grandpa Michael put all this information together. All he had was one of those old-fashioned laptop computers that they used in those days. Sez here that Giuseppe was found in the church "wheel" and that Giovanni did come back for Frances.

Chapter 23
Top Gun

More than half of York International's business was done outside the United States. To support this business, the company had sales, service, and manufacturing locations of one type or another in almost every country in the world. It was, therefore, incumbent on York's CEO to regularly visit many of these locations to see what was going on, to communicate the company's strategic plans, and to show employees at the site that they were an important part of York's business.

Business-related travel was continuous: by the time I had visited all major locations, it was necessary to start the cycle all over again. And since the travel that was required was in no way seasonal, there was almost never a time that I didn't have a business trip planned. It was hard work, but extraordinarily rewarding; there was no part of my job that I found more interesting.

Domestic travel was relatively easy because I usually had the company jet at my disposal. But international travel had to be done on commercial aircraft; the company plane did not have the range to take it outside North America. Fortunately, the company's pilots were skilled and a barrel of fun to be around. Once our chief pilot gave me brief verbal instructions on how to fly the airplane in case of an emergency. "It's very simple," he said. "Pull back on the wheel and the houses get smaller; push forward on the wheel and the houses get bigger. Unless you're upside down; then things are reversed."

You can be sure that I always saw to it that our pilots were well compensated for their services. Didn't want them worrying about their mortgage payments at 36,000 feet while they were trying to fly around a thunderstorm. As a side note, I also always took special care of our corporate vice president of human resources and my executive assistant. They were certainly talented individuals, but of greater importance, they were in positions of influence that could greatly affect my future. Giving them "favored nation" status helped me sleep well at night.

One of York's most important operations was the former Evcon facility in Wichita, Kansas. That was one of the businesses in which I had prior ownership before selling it to York. I had retained a home and a large parcel of land in Wichita after the business was sold, so I had a place to stay when I was in the city. I was visiting the Wichita facility at the time the World Trade Center was hit on September 11, 2001. As I was getting dressed on the morning of the attack, my phone rang: my assistant was calling to alert me to the events that were unfolding.

Because of the uncertainty surrounding the attack, all planes were prohibited from flying in US airspace for a period following the attack. That left me stranded in Wichita because both private and commercial aircraft were grounded. As it turned out, the first aircraft that were permitted to fly after the grounding were chartered aircraft; private planes and commercial planes remained grounded. A chartered aircraft was booked to fly me back to York as soon as permission to fly was granted.

The weather on the day of the return flight to York was unsettled across most of the country. Unfortunately, the aircraft that I was flying on was a turboprop, not a jet, which meant we were unable to fly over some of the worst weather we encountered. As we were approaching Harrisburg, Pennsylvania, our final destination, a thunderstorm was moving in from the north. The pilot decided that he needed to change course and fly south to avoid the storm.

What I didn't know at the time was that air traffic control had prohibited any aircraft on that first flying day from heading in the direction of Washington, DC. My pilot's repeated request to change course so that he could avoid the thunderstorm had been emphatically denied. In spite of that, my pilot headed south anyway, right toward Washington, DC. Air traffic control subsequently alerted the US military, which then scrambled several F-16 jets to intercept us.

I was unaware during the flight that there was a problem, but when we landed we were met by government officials who told us that we had come close to being shot down by the F-16s. All of a

sudden it was clear to me why my pilot looked and acted so harried after we landed. I didn't know it at the time but several F-16s had been right on our tail for the last portion of our trip. The story made the front page of the newspaper, but to this day I still don't know just how close we came to really being shot down.

Seems like there are an endless number of travel-related stories to tell, but most of them relate to the seemingly countless international trips that I have taken. I don't know how many times I got off an all-night flight and then headed straight to one of our business locations for an all-day meeting, followed by a dinner that seemed to last most of the night. Sometimes I had to struggle mightily to keep my eyes open because I was never able to get any sleep on the plane. And since I was the guest of honor at these affairs, I was always in the spotlight. There was no way to nod off without being noticed.

The upside to these trips was that key York personnel from the facility I was visiting were always there to pick me up at the airport, transport me around, make hotel reservations, take me to dinner, and show me the sights. All the fun, with little of the hassle; first-class treatment in every way. Sure did come to miss that in the extensive travel that I did after retirement.

Frequently when I traveled for York, I had a chance to meet with interesting dignitaries who were affiliated with the government or our customers and suppliers in the region. In Guangzhou, China, York was in partnership with the city government, so the distinguished mayor, the local politicians, and the press corps would frequently show up for a ceremonial dinner meeting. Politicians always seemed to know how important it was to get on the front page of the local newspapers.

Once at a dinner meeting in Kuala Lumpur, Malaysia, we had a scheduled meeting with a wealthy and politically well-connected businessman from the area. When we arrived at the designated hotel/restaurant we could hardly believe what we saw. An armed security force of at least a dozen bodyguards carrying machine guns was stationed in and around the restaurant and hotel lobby. We were told that an assault or a kidnapping was a threat, and that strong security measures were necessary. That was an uncomfortable meeting, to say the least.

Working for York allowed me to see much of the world: Asia Pacific; South Asia; the South Pacific; Western, Central, and Eastern Europe; the Scandinavian countries; South America; and the

Middle East. Most of that travel was uneventful, but there were times when flights were canceled and I was unable to rebook a suitable alternate flight.

Once in Thailand a hundred-dollar bill placed discreetly under an airline ticket for a canceled flight got me rebooked on another flight that was already fully booked. On a couple of other occasions, that approach met with criticism. Oh well, at least it worked once.

One of those rejections came when I was attempting to rebook a flight from Kuala Lumpur to Singapore. After that failed attempt, I was forced to hire a car and driver to make the trip. Everything was going fine until my driver was cut off by a truck while we were on the freeway that passes through the rubber plantations in southern Malaysia. At well over one hundred miles per hour we did a 360-degree spinout but were fortunate enough to avoid hitting anything.

Tell me again; how many chances do I get?

And while we're on the subject of chances, I've just got to tell you about the one-in-a-million opportunity that I had to fly on an F-16 fighter jet. It all came about as a result of having the winning bid at a fund-raiser auction for the Girls Club in Bristol, Tennessee, in early 2000. The item that was up for bid was an all-expenses-paid vacation trip to some exotic destination, I can't remember where. The bid for the trip was stalled at some relatively low number, to the disappointment of all, when a highly placed military man, a general, came up to the microphone and unexpectedly announced that he was going to add to the vacation package a flight on an Air Force F-16 fighter plane.

Are you serious? How in the hell is he able to do that? This guy must have some real pull.

Sure enough, the bidding took off like a rocket, or maybe I should say like an F-16. Higher and higher it went until it was down to me and only one other bidder. He bid, I bid, he bid, I bid, he bid…but I was determined.

The hard part, as it turned out, wasn't the bidding; actually getting the ride scheduled seemed to take forever. But my persistence paid off; about a year later I was off to Shaw Air Force Base in South Carolina for the experience of a lifetime.

I was told that I should arrive one day before the scheduled flight for prerequisite safety training. When I showed up at the base I was greeted like royalty. That evening all of the top brass and all of the fighter pilots attended a dinner in my honor. I didn't know why I was being treated with such high regard; none of these guys knew anything about me. But, what the hell, if that's what they wanted to do, so be it.

That first day of safety training was a blur. So much information was communicated that I soon realized I could only hope nothing went wrong during the flight; there was no way I would remember many of the actions that had to be taken in an emergency situation.

You'll be flying on a Block 40 F-16 training aircraft that has been modified to accommodate two seats. This is how all the seat belts are fastened. This is how you will communicate with the pilot by radio. These are the instruments that you will see in the cockpit in front of you. This is how the pressure suit works. This is how you restart the oxygen if necessary. The numerous buttons and levers that you see around you do the following things…

If there's a malfunction of the aircraft, pull the handle positioned right between your legs. If you do, both you and the pilot will be blasted out of the plane to parachute back to the ground. By the way, the ejection process is very violent. Make sure you don't pull the handle by accident because ejection does not require a concurrent action by the pilot. You pull it and you're both gone!

And just to be sure you don't end up with a tangled parachute line in case of an ejection, we're going to suspend you from the high ceiling in one of our hangars with a virtual reality helmet on so that you can practice reaching up over your head to untangle the lines if necessary.

Then I was in for a big surprise. The pilot who qualified as the top gun at the base was going to fly with me, not someone of lesser ability. He was the best of the best. What a character: confident, cocky, physically exceptional, obviously highly intelligent, athletic. In a lot of ways, just like me…just kidding…or am I?

The biggest surprise of all was his offer to put me through all thirteen top-gun competition maneuvers, not just some pansy-ass, simple up and down flight like Grandma would go on. Did I want that kind of ride was the question.

You bet!

Okay then, if that's what you want, that's what I'll give you. And by the way, there are thirteen more advanced top-gun competition maneuvers that we can also do, if you're up to it. That would be a total of twenty-six maneuvers. What do you think?

If I'm up to it? You can bet your ass!

Okay, we're at the end of the runway and this top-gun hotshot wants to impress me. Full afterburners are on and we're accelerating at a phenomenal rate. Liftoff, and we're soon going straight up, over the top, and upside down. But you ain't seen nothin' yet. Spins, dives, extreme turns with the wings perpendicular to the ground, more upside-down flying, loops…we did it all. Twenty-six competition maneuvers, all at the full limits of the plane's and the pilot's capability. After each maneuver the top-gun hotshot asked me if I wanted to continue on to the next one.

Y…o…u…b…e…t…!

The last thing we did was something he called cloud dodging. This was not a competition maneuver; rather, it was flying around the numerous puffy clouds that happened to be dotting the sky that day. The game was to fly at a high speed around the clouds without entering them. The challenge came in not being able to see the next cloud until we had gotten around the cloud that was nearest to us. That required extraordinary maneuvering as we weaved in and out, and up and down around the clouds.

As we were heading back to the base, Top Gun commented that he knew that I was well connected to Donald Rumsfeld, then the secretary of defense, and asked what kind of guy he was.

Me? Well connected to Donald Rumsfeld? Oh my god… that's why I had gotten the royal treatment. They expected that I would be a conduit to the top man in the defense department. But I didn't know the man at all…never even met him. I surmised that the general who added this flight to the auction, the guy who set this whole thing up, had told the base that I was some well-connected big shot so he could get me the flight.

Ahhhh…yeah…he's a really great guy…can't wait to tell him all about this experience.

I left the base that day with a signed certificate that said I had experienced 9.5 g's, which is near the limit that a human being can tolerate. Even though we had done all of the full competition maneuvers, I hadn't gotten sick, but my head was spinning for at least a week afterwards.

And I had every intention of telling Donald Rumsfeld about my wonderful experience, if and when I ever met the man.

Chapter 24

La vie en rose

When you stop to think about it, every relationship I was ever in ended or failed for one reason or another. Some survived far longer than others, but none went the distance. And the last one was the hardest of all to try to get over. "To try to get over" is the right way to say it because it was definitely not yet behind me. With that kind of track record, there was little reason to think anything would ever change. Did I want to try it all over again, or was flying solo from then on the best idea of all?

At somewhere around age sixty-three I still thought that I had a lot more to do in my life. Not those lofty goals that were life's passions when I was young, but the fun things that require only that you show up to enjoy them. No hard work, no stress, no preparation required. Getting to that point in life had already happened, so it seemed like the time was right for me to turn in some of my coupons and walk away with a few more of the good times that were right there for the taking.

New York Review of Books Classified Ads

Male, early 60s, physically fit and in excellent health. Well edu-cated, very successful in business, and financially secure. Love sunlight, outdoors, music, performing arts, humor, intimacy, learning, and new experiences. Automotive enthusiast with good hands-on skills. Indepen-dent, intelligent, intellectual, intuitive, and inventive. Very well traveled with many interesting and diverse experiences. Not religious but have high ethical standards. Politically liberal with a sensitivity to the rights and needs of others. Have the wherewithal to deal with life's challenges. Try to understate but exceed expectations. Seeking...

Okay, let's see if anyone responds to this ad.

There's one, there's another, and another. Twenty-eight, twenty-nine, thirty, and they are still coming. But it's not just the quantity that matters, it's the quality that's most important.

...composer, doctor, journalist, film director, professor, law-yer...hmmm...better stay away from that last one...actually, other than that, not really a bad one in the group.

No, maybe, no, no, no, no, no, maybe...

Wow, this one's really interesting: English professor, Yale PhD, author, good-looking, and lives in Minneapolis, one of the few places you can get to from Wichita without a plane change.

Okay, when we meet in New York I'll bring you a couple of

CDs that I've made of some of my favorite music. Can't wait to meet you.

Well, my favorite book is *Grapes of Wrath*. Not saying that it's the best book ever written, just saying that it's one that made a lasting impression on me. *High Noon* is my favorite movie; nothing else comes close. *Death of a Salesman* knocked me over when I saw it on Broadway. *Lucia di Lammermoor* is my favorite opera. *Giselle* is my favorite ballet. "Once Upon a Time" is my favorite song. My favorite painting/illustration is "Reflections" by Lee Teter. You've got to look that one up if you are not already familiar with it.

Travel has been a big part of my life. Seen all the states and most foreign countries. Some of that travel was work-related, but much has been to interesting places that I wanted to see on my own. No question about it, being outdoors, preferably on property that I own, is one of my favorite things to do. Just put me under a shady tree out on the Kansas prairie, preferably with a book in my hands, and I'm a happy man.

Opera, symphonies, rock concerts, recorded music, Broadway plays, museums, movies, travel, good books, sporting events…so you like those things too, eh? Everything except the sports stuff, you say? Well then, why don't we give it a try?

This is really something; she knows at least as much about these museum exhibits as I do, probably more. Now that's a change. And she's read all the books that that author has written; I've only read two of them. And she seemed to enjoy that opera at the Met just as much as I did. That's a good sign. Hmmm…there's a lot to like here.

You know, with a name as beautiful as Madelon Marie, I can't understand why anyone would call you Mimi. I'm not going to do that. You're Madelon Marie…that's a lot nicer.

So what parts of Italy are you planning to see? Venice, Padua, and Florence…yes, I've been there quite a few times, and I've always enjoyed it. York International had a manufacturing plant and widespread sales operations in Italy…

Yes, I will join you. Any chance we could also dip farther south in the direction of Rome so that I could visit the towns that my mother's parents were from? Isola del Liri and Sora. That would be the highlight of the trip for me.

So you're saying that the Scrovegni Chapel in Padua has a remarkable collection of frescoes created by Giotto around 1300, eh? And you're saying it was commissioned by Enrico degli Scrovegni, a wealthy banker, as a private chapel for his family? Oh yeah, guess I knew that…must have just slipped my mind.

Sure do appreciate your willingness to go with me to Isola del Liri and Sora. Getting a chance to see where my mother's parents lived meant everything to me, but sharing that experience with you made all the difference, and the subject of another story.

This is really something; she knows at least as much about

Italy as I do, probably more. Now that's a change. Never had this much fun traveling with anyone else before. Hmmm…there's a lot to like here.

The home and building that you see will be the focal point of this fourteen-hundred-acre parcel. Just try to picture this after it undergoes a complete transformation. All those old cars and trucks in the back will be gone, and so will the enclosure that's being used up front for the two burros. I'm going to completely redo the inside finished area. The ceiling upstairs will be ten feet high, and there will be nothing but windows on all three of the outside walls. I'm going to put in oak trim around all the windows and doors with matching base and crown molding. That stairway will be opened up and a handrail that complements the rest of the trim carpentry will be installed.

You'll see, it will be complete in about a year.

I'm glad you like being out here as much as I do. Sometimes getting away from everything allows you to clear your head and refocus on what's really important in life. Let's start our walk today toward the wooded area to the south, then west to the farthest prairie area, then past the four large ponds near the center of the property, and then head back to the house. About eight miles, so we should be back in about three hours if we stop along the way to enjoy things.

From that desk you have a panoramic view of the outside through all the windows that surround you. I can't think of anyplace that's more conducive to writing. For the next few days we can both work on our writing and then sit outside on the patio at night to enjoy the Kansas sky. You know, when I think about what folks living in the big city are missing I can only assume that they just don't know that there's another way to live.

What I like most about being with you is that we both enjoy so many different things: a Rolling Stones concert in Wichita, the Russian museum in Minneapolis, walking around New York City, a night out for dinner and a movie, or just time spent together reading. I really like when you read aloud and then we follow that up with a discussion of the book: Churchill, Franklin, Darwin, Einstein, Jefferson, Peter the Great, *War and Peace, Lawrence (In) Arabia…*

A little of this, a little of that: Kansas prairie today, Wichita tomorrow, Minneapolis the next time I come up to see you.

Minneapolis, what a great place to be. For a city that's not on one of the coasts, it's got a lot to offer. Performing arts, the Mississippi River, gorgeous homes, lakes, trees…and everything is so well maintained. And talk about beautiful homes: yours is just about perfect. Well over one hundred years old and probably in better shape now than it's ever been. High ceilings, beautiful woodwork, and an outside presence that makes it stand out from the rest.

So why don't we get a little more adventurous the next time we travel? After we stop in England to see your grandchildren get christened, we can head to Central Europe to see what Bulgaria, Romania, and Hungary are like. That would be a lot more fun, I think, than just going back to one of the old hangouts. Nothing much new or challenging in retracing those well-worn steps, is there?

Flew into Varna on the Black Sea, trained across country to Bucharest, then farther on to Brasov, and still farther to Budapest. What an experience. But I think the best part of that trip was stumbling in on that a cappella group that we heard while we were walking around town in Brasov. Glad we took the chance and followed the music into the building and up the stairs. Never would have guessed that they would invite us into the room that they were using to rehearse. No doubt about it, I had never heard anything so beautiful in my life: just sitting there, right in the midst of such wonderful voices. Without question, one of my most memorable experiences.

Vietnam, Laos, and Cambodia…now that was a trip I'd been wanting to take for a long time. By the third night in Hanoi we pretty well had the city figured out. Not sure how far we walked that night, but it had to be well over ten miles. Glad we were both up for that.

Just had to see the Balkans too. Serbia, Croatia, Slovenia, Bosnia, Montenegro, Macedonia, and Kosovo, all the former Yugoslav states, were so different from each other that it made sense to hire a car and driver to take us all through the region, and then into Albania, too.

The Czech Republic, Slovakia, Ukraine, Belarus, and Russia came next. Could have spent a month in St. Petersburg and still not seen it all. What a circus.

Then France, the tip of Italy, and England to give my granddaughter a little international exposure. Guess she was too young to get much out of it, though; too bad.

But Madelon Marie and I were back on our own adventures the next year. Wanted to see what Poland, Lithuania, and Latvia were all about. The Treblinka concentration camp was horrific; no surprise there.

Following that we were off to Armenia, Georgia, Azerbaijan, Iran, and Turkey. Now that was a real ass kicker, but possibly the best of all the trips we'd taken. Never met a more welcoming group of people than the Iranians. How is it possible that Americans have such negative feelings toward Iran?

Almost running out of countries. Not sure what comes after Portugal and Morocco and a revisit to Spain, but you can be sure that I'll keep traveling right up to the end of my days. But hopefully that end is still quite a way off.

Sometimes relationships take off like a rocket, reach maximum altitude, and then plummet back to earth in a pile of rubble. Other times they can lift off the ground, reach a cruising altitude, and then gently glide back to earth and land. All passengers disembark safely and head off in different directions. Most often, they try to take off but can't seem to reach liftoff speed, so they end up stopping at the end of the runway. Everyone on board gets on the next flight, hoping that that will be the one to reach its destination. On rare occasions a relationship will take off, reach orbital altitude, and stay aloft for a lifetime. For that to happen, a lot of things all have to work right and meld together.

How fortunate I was that my relationship with Madelon Marie had turned into love that seemed likely to last a lifetime. In almost every way we fit perfectly together. Both of us adventurous, both with widely varying interests, and both conversant on a wide variety of subjects. No roller-coaster rides or wrestling matches, just an attraction that constantly grew stronger with time.

So, Madelon Marie, think of me, even if I'm gone, when you hear your song:

La vie en rose

Hold me close and hold me fast
The magic spell you cast
This is la vie en rose

When you kiss me heaven sighs
And though I close my eyes
I see la vie en rose

When you press me to your heart
I'm in a world apart
A world where roses bloom

And when you speak, angels sing from above
Everyday words seem to turn into love songs

Give your heart and soul to me
And life will always be la vie en rose

Sung by Cindi Lauper

Chapter 25
City Boy

The war was over, my dad had finally been discharged, and we were temporarily living with my grandmother in Detroit. It was time for our family to take a big step in our quest for independence: buy our own home. I wasn't aware of it at the time, but for several months in late 1949 my parents had been searching for a place that we could call our own. Middle, middle-class families like ours certainly couldn't afford anything more than the most basic of starter homes, so a brand-new, single-bath, three-bedroom, story-and-a-half bungalow in the emerging near northern Detroit suburb of Royal Oak was soon to become our dream home.

Homes similar to ours were being built by the tens of thousands to accommodate the servicemen who had returned home with the GI Bill in one hand and a wife and kids, or a sweetheart, in the other. They were young and ambitious, needed a place to live, and in many cases were seeking a college education. Housing and education, that's what the GI Bill helped to provide honorably discharged servicemen. That was who we were; that was our family.

The small lot that our home was on was bordered on one side by an easement property that was never going to be used by the city for its originally intended purpose, so we had the good fortune to have a somewhat premium lot in the neighborhood. Still postage-stamp size, but slightly bigger than the lots that surrounded us. But there was no doubt about it, we were city slickers in the truest sense. That was fine by me. I didn't know there was any other way to live.

Farm life? Man oh man, who would ever want that? No stores close enough to reach by bicycle; what good was that? No kids living close by; who were you going to play football with? Those farm people, from the little exposure that I had to them, seemed to be different from us in so many ways.

Perhaps my first exposure to farm life came when I was about four years old. My mother's sister Ann had married a guy named Marvin, a gruff and unpolished farmer who really freaked me out. One day while I was staying with them over a weekend, Marvin offered to take me for a ride on his tractor while he plowed one of his fields. At that age I had no say in the matter; my protests fell on deaf ears; I was a human being without any measure of human rights. As I sat there on the tractor seat with Marvin's arm tightly around my waist, my fear turned to terror when the tractor started up with a deafening roar. The tractor had no engine muffler, and the exhaust pipe that came straight up from the engine seemed to blow right in our faces. I was terrified; Marvin thought it was funny. Finally, my aunt persuaded him to end the ride and let me go.

I didn't know any swear words at that time, so there was no way that I could express how I really felt. But you stupid ass would have been a good start. Any wonder why I started out hating farm life?

That first farm experience was followed by one that left a different but equally long lasting impression. We were visiting another one of my mother's siblings, my uncle Ted, who lived on a small farm outside the city. Ted wasn't really a bad guy, but he was stern, loud-spoken, and opinionated. No problem with that; at least he never tried to force me to join him on one of his tractor rides. On this particular visit my brother and my cousins and I decided to play hide-and-seek.

The small farm provided a lot of great places to hide, so in that sense it was an ideal place to play the game. As we all ran off to hide, I spotted what appeared to be a water well, or something of that nature, not too far from the house. It was enclosed by a circular brick wall about eight feet in diameter and about two feet tall, had a flat concrete floor, and was capped with a roof enclosure. It wasn't a water well, but from a distance it looked just like one. As I now think back, it was probably a storage bin for some type of grain that was grown on the farm.

I rolled myself over the edge of the enclosure and lay on my stomach, flat on the floor, with the side of my face resting on the floor as well. I didn't move a muscle for the longest time. As long as I remained perfectly flat no one could find me. What a great hiding place…or was it?

As I was lying there, I eventually came to realize that something was moving all around me. I felt it on my face, my hands, my stomach, my feet, everywhere. What was going on? Then I looked more closely at the floor I was lying on, and to my horror I realized that beneath a fine layer of dust the entire floor was covered in maggots. Wall to wall, maggot to maggot, they were everywhere. My face, my hands, my feet, my entire body, all in an enormous sea of maggots. Oh my god! I couldn't think of anything worse than lying in a sea of maggots.

No, my first farm experiences did not leave me with warm and fuzzy feelings that would likely keep me coming back for more. Not warm and fuzzy; more like creepy, crawly, loud, and scary. It's no

wonder that for most of the rest of my life I didn't find much that was interesting in farm life or farm land. It's funny, though, that this didn't make me dislike outdoor life in general. Woods, parks, and all other outdoor experiences were always a great attraction to me. But show me something with an old farmhouse and a tractor on it, and I would invariably turn off.

It wasn't until much later that I would decide to purchase two relatively small parcels of land in Bristol, Tennessee. The first was several acres of elevated land that overlooked South Holston Lake; the second was a sixty-acre parcel of land just outside the city limits. Owning land was a new experience for me, but one that I really came to like. Unfortunately, we left the Bristol area and sold the land long before I was able to fully appreciate the experience of being a landowner. But my appetite had been whetted: not to be a farmer, but maybe a land baron. Hmmm…

Showed up in Wichita, Kansas, in the spring of 1991 with nothing more than a suitcase and the keys to the front door of Evcon Industries. I didn't know a single person in town, how the city was laid out, or where I wanted to live. Just before arriving in Wichita, I called the information operator and asked if she would give me the name and phone number of the real estate firm that had the largest display ad in the local phone book. That's how I started my time in Wichita: everything was new to me.

Three years and two homes later, I kind of had things figured out. Business was good and I had come to like Wichita. I know, you're probably thinking to yourself, Wichita, Kansas, what's to like there? Actually, there's a lot to like in Wichita: friendly people, mostly sunny skies, decent weather, and the magnificent great plains, for starters. A city large enough to accommodate virtually all of your everyday needs without the traffic jams or high cost of living of New York, Chicago, or San Francisco. How anyone could put up with that kind of big-city turmoil every day has been a mystery to me ever since I first left suburban Detroit.

When my second-oldest son, Alex, and his fiancée, Joni, decided to build a home, they looked at vacant land that was then several miles outside the Wichita city limits. Their search subsequently led me to discover a 160-acre quarter section of land that was for sale. Soon I was a landowner once again. It seemed like I was out in the middle of nowhere because the area had not yet seen much development. About two years later I would also purchase the adjoining 160-acre quarter section of land that was directly east of the first piece that I had purchased. Today, that land is still my primary residence, but I'm now surrounded by the city. After twenty-plus years of hard work, I'm fortunate to now have one of the most beautiful pieces of land in the area.

Much has happened since I acquired the first parcels of land in the Wichita area. I've increased my land interests to over three thousand acres. Most of my free time is spent overseeing various activities related to improvement of the land: fence removal and replacement, pond dredging, tree trimming and removal, bush cutting, bridge building, and a lot more are year-around activities. Most farmers don't have the time or the inclination to do much of what I do because farming is a business to them. That I understand. But my focus is on improving the land in every way possible. Since I don't need to make a living from the land, my singular objective is to enjoy it.

Turn me loose on one of my ATVs and I'll find my way to one of the most beautiful spots on one of the eight major parcels. Be it in a wooded area, by a pond, or right in the middle of a vast stretch of prairie, I'll be in my element, often with a book in my hand. How could anyone not love a farm?

But no story is complete without an element of humor. This incident occurred shortly after my first land purchases.

On that particular summer's day I had driven out to see what progress had been made on two homes that our family was building on our newly acquired land. Shortly after arriving, I decided to take a walk to the far side of the property. When I was approximately three-quarters of a mile from the new home sites and from my pickup truck, I felt a firm pat on my ass from what I immediately assumed was someone who had quietly snuck up on me from behind. Not funny, I thought as I turned around to confront the jokester.

To my surprise there was no one behind me, but there was something else...a huge cougar (mountain lion/panther). That's what had nudged me with its head. The last thing that I ever would have expected to see was a cougar, especially one that probably weighed over 170 pounds, had teeth that were somewhere around

three inches long, and claws that looked like daggers. Eye to eye we stood looking at each other. I didn't move; it didn't move. Was this thing about to attack? What to do?

Start walking back to my pickup truck; no other option. But it was a long walk back, and the cougar walked with me every step of the way. At no time did it appear ready to attack, but along the way I found a tree limb that I picked up to use as a club if that became necessary. Okay, kitty, it's just you and me now; are you going to start something?

Ten minutes seemed like an hour. As I climbed back into my vehicle, I gave a sigh of relief before turning my attention to calling the police department. The cat had decided to lie down right beside my vehicle, which seemed strange. But there it stayed, and there it was when the police car finally showed up. With our windows down, the two of us communicated. It wasn't long before the cop heard over his radio that the cougar had escaped from someone in the area who was keeping it as a pet. A pet cougar?

After over an hour of waiting, the cougar's owner still hadn't shown up. My main concern was that if the cat was not recaptured it might show up some day when I was out again on my property. Constantly having to look over my shoulder was the last thing I wanted to do, so recapture was imperative. After lying beside our vehicles for more than an hour, the cougar finally got up and began to walk slowly behind one of the homes that was under construction. The cop got out of his car and followed, gun drawn, arms outstretched, and aiming at the animal. I got out of my truck and followed him as he followed the cat.

When we got behind the home, the cat turned around and approached us in a somewhat intimidating manner. Wasn't sure if it was going to attack us, but for the first time that appeared to be a real possibility. Why in the hell I had gotten out of the car to follow the cop, who was following the cat, wasn't at all clear to me then.

The cop was petrified and began yelling at the cat to stop, as if it were a person who could understand what he was saying. "Stop, or I'll shoot! Don't come any closer! Stop! Stop!" Even then, in the midst of a potentially serious encounter, I realized how ridiculous the whole thing had become. I was certain the cop was going to shoot. The cat paused. Perhaps it did understand the English language after all. We both slowly backed up to the safety of our vehicles. Let's just let the damn thing wander off!

Finally, the owner showed up in his pickup truck with the animal's cage in the back. After a brief search, the cat was found near the home, but it took the owner at least an hour to coax it close enough so that it could be re-collared and led back to its cage. By that time a reporter for the local newspaper had arrived; how he had heard about the ordeal I didn't know. The next day the story was page-one news and I was a local hero, for one day at least.

Encountering a cougar is probably less likely than being struck by lightning. Encountering two cougars in a single lifetime is undoubtedly off the probability charts. Well, you already may have guessed that I'm going to tell you that that's exactly what happened to me.

Several years after my first encounter I was considering the purchase of a large parcel of land about forty miles outside Wichita. I revisited the land numerous times so that I could familiarize myself with every aspect of the property. This was a primitive parcel with large ponds, heavy trees, and wide-ranging grassy areas. I was inclined to purchase the property, but I wanted a second opinion, so I asked my brother Gordy if he would look it over and tell me what he thought.

Later that Sunday evening I got a call from my brother. "Mike," he said, "when Debi and I were leaving the property a cougar crossed the road right in front of us. You need to be careful when you're out there. We both saw it, and we're certain that it was a cougar." All I could think of was that they had seen a deer, or some other animal, and mistook it for a cougar. There weren't supposed to be any cougars in Kansas, or at least any reported sightings were thought to be incorrect. There were cougars in the neighboring state of Colorado, but nothing in Kansas. That was the official word on the subject.

When I next returned to the property, the thought of a cougar didn't even cross my mind because I was sure my brother and his wife must have been mistaken. But as I was driving my ATV on a desolate portion of the property, far from my pickup truck, I noticed something about one hundred feet ahead of me that was running across my path. My first thought was that it was probably a deer, but when I took a good look at it I realized that it was a cougar. When it got right in front of me, it turned toward me and stopped. I stopped. There we were, staring at each other, neither one of us moving. Déjà vu.

Now what was I going to do? If I took off in the opposite direction, the cat would probably think the chase was on, and since I was sure my vehicle couldn't outrun it, that seemed like a bad idea. We sat there looking at each other for at least a minute. I didn't know what to do. Then the cougar walked off in the direction that it had been heading before the encounter. Okay, I thought, but now how was I going to get back to my vehicle? The

possibility of a second encounter as I crossed the property was real, but what else was I going to do? Slowly I drove back to my truck so as to not upset the cat if I did cross its path again. When I later stopped by the sheriff's office to report the incident he listened to my story and then said there were no cougars in Kansas, but he admitted that there had been several unverified sightings.

On four subsequent occasions I saw the cat again from the safety of my vehicle. Three of those times I was with another person, so there can be no question as to my sanity. I didn't buy the property…even though I'd been assured and reassured that there were no cougars in Kansas!

Chapter 26

Can't Buy It

A bearded man in a white robe, raising the dead, walking across the water, and turning water into wine...

I can't buy it.

Agnostic is the word; you know that *other word* is so hard for people to deal with that it's better left unsaid. So we won't say it; we'll just say agnostic instead.

Sure wish the story was true, though. I really do. I don't want my existence to end when I die; I want it to go on for eternity. I really do. But wishing something doesn't turn it into reality, no matter how hard you want it. So we have to come to grips with the reality of our situations. This is probably all there is; ain't no more, no how, no way.

I say *probably* because I don't claim to understand many extraordinary concepts like infinite time and space or the origins of life, to name a few. So there might be more to the story, but that fact alone does not entitle us to create a fictitious explanation for what we don't understand, just so that we can sleep at night.

And which version of the story are we to believe, anyway? Does Christianity have it right? How about Islam, Judaism, Hinduism, Jainism, Buddhism, Sikhism, Taoism, Confucianism, Shintoism, or Zoroastrianism? Or how about one of those ancient religions that we hardly even know about today? And which one of the gods are we to believe in? Brahma, Rama, Krishna, Vishnu, Maheswara, Shiva, Allah, Quetzalcoatl, Biame, Jupiter, Zeus, Breged, Ahura Mazda, or one of the other gods of ancient religions?

But, you interrupt, those other religions had it all wrong. We've got it right, and we've got a religious book to prove it!

Really? But I thought those other religions had religious books of their own that showed that they were right, too.

No, you say, those books weren't authentic. Ours is the right one!

But they say that, too.

I know, but believe me, we're right and they are wrong. In fact, countless numbers of our believers have died for our belief because they knew that we were right!

But they have, too.

You know that there's just no sense talking about this anymore. You nonbelievers are all alike. You'll just never understand.

That's one thing that you are right about; I'll just never understand.

All right, you say, I'll give it one more try. How do you nonbelievers explain the creation of the universe? How do you explain the limitless bounds of space? How did the earth come into being if it wasn't created by God? You don't have an answer, do you?

That's right, I don't have an answer. But that doesn't mean that there is anything supernatural about it. Just because we don't yet understand something doesn't mean that it will always be unknowable. It just means that our human minds have not developed far enough for us to understand everything. Think of the cavemen who saw lightning and attributed it to a supernatural cause. They didn't yet understand the reality of the event. Someday, our minds may have developed far enough to comprehend what we do not now know.

So now I'll ask you a question.

Let's say I'm holding a large bag of marbles. You can't see what's in the bag because it is opaque, but you do know that there are thousands of marbles in the bag. Now I'll ask you to reach into the bag without looking and remove one marble. The marble turns out to be green. You then reach into the bag again and pull out another marble. That one turns out to be green as well. Let's repeat the process until you've removed several hundred or even several thousand marbles. If every single one of the marbles that you have removed is green, with no exceptions, what color do you think the next marble that you remove from the bag will be?

Of course it is possible that the next marble that comes out of the bag will be blue, but does that seem likely to you? If you asked thousands or even millions of others what color marble will likely be next to come out of the bag, you would be surprised if anyone answered blue, yellow, red, purple, or any color other than green.

And so I'll now ask you if every one of the thousands of religious beliefs prior to yours was wrong, why would you be surprised if I doubted that the next one in line, in this case yours, would finally be the right one?

What's the likelihood that after all those green marbles came out of the bag, the next one is going to be blue?

What's the likelihood that after all those other religious beliefs were wrong, the next one is going to be right?

Chapter 27
Close Your Eyes

HOW long does this process take, anyway? I've been waiting for more than seventy years and it hasn't happened yet. Could have happened when I got polio at age ten, but it didn't. They gave me the last rites, and all that, and then they told me everything was going to be all right. They didn't lie to me, did they? Yeah, I survived, but it really wasn't all right, was it? No, it never was. I survived and then I spent the rest of my life as a survivor. Fighting my way through it all. A survivor. Ma, you taught me how to do that, didn't you?

But I saw your red eyes and your tears even though you tried to hide them, Ma. And it seemed like your red eyes never, ever went away. Here, Ma, use these tissues, and let me put my arms around you to make it better. See, Ma, that's all it took. Nothing can hurt you now, Ma, and it can't hurt me either, right? But we never did much of that kind of thing did we? Not once we got a little bit older, anyway. Had to learn to be tough. Had to learn to get over it. That's how it's done, isn't it, Ma? Learn to get over it.

With all the gifts I've been given it's hard to understand what all this fuss is about. I really did experience just about all that life had to offer; much more than so many other people. So why am I so sad? That's a good question, isn't it? Guess it's because the gifts came with a pretty steep price tag: a sense from the earliest age of what reality really is. A deep understanding of how perilous life can be. Better look both ways before you step off the curb. Better hope that airplane lands safely. Better hope that beating heart of yours doesn't decide to take a vacation. Thump, thump, thump, thump, thump. Still going after all these years? Thump, thump, thump.

But now I'm so old. Clearly my best years are behind me. And when does the mental function start to decline? Almost certainly that process has begun, but at least I'm not aware of it yet. Ten more years? Twenty at the most. But then again it may be just a few minutes more. In a way that's the odd part. You just keep thinking about tomorrow, because as the song says, "you're only a day away." Seems so hard to believe that one day there won't be any tomorrow.

And I'll be all gone except for the ashes and the memories that linger in a few people's minds. *Oh yeah, I remember him; he was kind of an interesting guy. He once ran York International, I think. Or was it some other company? Anyway, pass me that celery dip, I'm famished.*

All gone? And what happens to all those experiences that I had in my life? The ones that I've been storing so carefully away in that overactive brain of mine. Where do the memories of those experiences go? Don't tell me they just disappear. No, don't tell

me that. The experiences that caused those memories were far too important for them to just disappear forever. You just don't understand how significant all those events were!

How did I survive it all so far? Probability theory, it seems, would have predicted that one of those possible life-threatening events would have caught up with me long before now. That gun that was held to my head during that motel robbery attempt in New Orleans. That airplane that almost turned over when it got caught in wind shear while trying to land in Washington, DC. The small passenger boat that was lost at night in dense fog with no navigation equipment or life jackets that managed to steer clear of countless rock formations protruding from Ha Long Bay. And all the bridges that never collapsed and the cars that never ran the red light to broadside me. Seems like the odds were a million to one against getting this far.

So, doc, you say that I've got major blockages in all the arteries that connect to my heart and that I need immediate bypass surgery? And I recently had a heart attack that apparently I didn't even know about? Actually, I thought that chest pain I experienced several months back had something to do with getting hit during a hockey game I had played in. Yeah, I'm still playing hockey at my ancient age. You ought to see me trying to keep up with some of these young guys. Sometimes I do put the puck in the back of the net, and every once in a great while I make a semi-spectacular play. In my opinion, anyway.

I can hear you. I can tell what you're saying. See, I'm moving my right foot. Can you see it? Look at how vigorously I'm moving my foot. I'm starting to wake up now. Guess I'm still alive because I can hear them all talking. They're telling me the bypass operation was a success and I'm going to be all right. There, they said it again, and again, and again. I'm going to be all right. They wouldn't lie to me, would they? No, everything isn't really going to be all right, is it? But I will be a survivor for a little while longer.

No problem, guys, the doctor told me that I could go back and do all the things I used to do before the surgery. Work your heart hard, he said; that's the best thing you can do for it.

Pass me the puck, I can beat this goalie with an upper corner shot on his stick side…

By the way, I'm going to miss a few games in August because we'll be traveling to the former Yugoslavia for several weeks.

Chapter 28
The Spirit Departs

This final chapter should have been written after my death, but for obvious reasons that couldn't be done unless someone else were to write it. Therein lies the problem: I want to say something about my death, an event that has not yet happened, and the details of which I do not yet know. I must, therefore, deal with this subject in the broadest possible way so that I can address the various end-of-life possibilities. Please bear with me on this; it is not my intention to be morbid, or for this to be upsetting. But, by its very nature, this subject is difficult to deal with.

I am now in my early seventies. There's no arguing with the fact that I don't have too much time left. That's okay, because I really don't want to go on for too much longer anyway. And if you gave me the chance to go back and do it all over again, I'd turn it down. It's just that I don't want to gradually fade off with disabilities or with declining mental capability. That hasn't happened to me yet, but there's no doubt that at some time in the future I'll have to deal with that eventuality, unless an accident or a sudden illness takes me first.

The possibility of gradually fading off, with events out of my control, is horrifying to me. I watched that happen to my parents, and to others along the way. But if I have any control over my end-of-life situation, I will not let that happen to me. So far, I've survived polio, a heart attack, quintuple bypass surgery, and who knows whatever else that could have brought about my demise. I think I'm now functioning about as well as most guys who are ten years younger than me, and for that I am grateful. I still play ice hockey four or more times per week with guys who are all younger than me, some less than one-third my age. To my good fortune, they continue to put up with an old man who tries his best to keep up with them. I love every minute of it, but I can tell that that activity will soon have to end. The fact is that I passed the point when I should have quit several years ago, but I've kept on going anyway.

The signs of decline are everywhere: minor chest pain, leaking heart valve, diminished kidney function: the inevitable is inevitable. I have absolutely no fear of dying, but I'm terrified of living, if my life were to be noticeably compromised. The real problem, though, is that if I were to take preemptive action, the impact on others would be devastating. And if I took that action before a disabling event occurred, it would be even harder for others to deal with.

I regret greatly that the country I live in makes it virtually impossible to end life, if that is deemed necessary, in a planned and dignified manner, with friends and family present. I wouldn't think of trying to tell others what their end-of-life scenario should be, so where do others get off trying to tell *me* what *not* to do? I've had the medication for years. I've read the books. I've seen the videos.

If the day comes when I need to act proactively, I have every intention, and every right, to do so.

I say all this for one simple reason: I want my family and friends, anyone who might know me, to understand that if the time comes when I must bring things to an end, I will do it with no regrets whatsoever, that I would not have been able to tell them beforehand what was about to happen, and that there would have been no way that I could have ever said good-bye.

What worries me greatly is that people might then think to themselves that I must have had an unhappy life, that I was depressed, that I didn't value life, or that I must not have cared about them. Nothing would be further from the truth. I've been extremely fortunate; I've had a great life; I've almost done it all. No one ever could have asked for more.

Final Thoughts

It's Sunday, January 29, 2:20 p.m., and I'm sitting in a beautiful wooded area in Wichita, Kansas on a spectacular warm mid winter day. I know exactly how I got here. I started out as a Michigan boy but now more than half my life has been spent in other states.

I live with my terrific wife, Vicki, who came into my life recently, and unexpectedly. I'd say that I was a very lucky man, but then again, someone this good just doesn't come along by accident. I've worked hard to get where I am, and I feel entitled to have someone this special in my life.

Some way or another I've managed to remain close to the top of my game. I hope I can keep this up for a long time to come. Really enjoyed the trip to New Zealand that we took several months ago, got four hockey games I'll be playing in this week, and have a trip to Capri, Pompeii, and Sicily next month.

Tomorrow is supposed to be another warm and sunny day; planning to put the top down on my Corvette so that I can sneak a little more sunshine into my life.

I don't think it gets any better than this.